So you really want to learn

Spanish

BOOK 1

So you really want to learn

Spanish

BOOK 1

Mike Bolger B.A., M.I.L.
Series Editor: Nicholas Oulton M.A. (Oxon.)

GALORE PARK

Published by Galore Park Publishing Ltd.,
19/21 Sayers Lane, Tenterden, Kent TN30 6BW

Text copyright © Mike Bolger 2003
Illustrations copyright © Galore Park 2003
Typography and layout by Typetechnique, London W1
Printed and bound in India by Replika Press Pvt. Ltd.

ISBN: 978 1 902984 10 0

First published 2003, reprinted 2008, 2011, 2012

Details of other Galore Park publications are available at
www.galorepark.co.uk

ISEB Revision Guides, publications and examination papers
may also be obtained from Galore Park.

Acknowledgements

The publishers would like to thank the many generous people, without whose help the production of this book, and the resources that accompany it, would have been impossible. In particular they would like to thank Janet Beloso for her tireless work in producing a large number of the exercises. Special thanks are also due to:

Simon Craft, Elena de Celis, Ann Buxade del Tronco, Evelyn Shellard, Vanessa Fleitas Diaz, Cinta Romero, Peter Such, Keith Hannis, Alfredo Bello, Laura Vargas Llanas, Sara Foster, Maria Vidler, Maite Ross-Skedd, Carmen Brown, Andina Brown, Rosi Parker, Elena Peck, Miguel Alemany, Bella Griffith, Nick Griffith, Imanol Etxeberria, Tom and Alistair Davis, Richard Studholme, Tim Green, the "Spanish guitarist" at the Tone Zone Studio, Kevin Dodd, Emma Oulton, Sophie Oulton and Caterina Busquets.

Illustrations and Photos

The 3-D cartoons used in this book are © www.animationfactory.com. Additional drawings were supplied by Graham Edwards.

All the photographs were supplied by Turespaña, except those on page 47, which were supplied by El Juli (www.eljuli.com).

Preface

Spanish is spoken by more than 450 million people across the world, from the Philippines in the east to Peru in the west. More people in America now speak Spanish than they do English. And as a holiday destination, Spain has it all: sun, sand, snow-topped mountains, lush green meadows, delicious food and wine – you name it, Spain has it. So all you have to do now is learn Spanish; and if you *really* want to learn Spanish, this is the book for you!

Contents

UNIT 1 – ¡Hola!

UNIT 2 – La familia y los amigos

UNIT 3 – El horario

UNIT 4 – En casa

UNIT 5 – En el pueblo

UNIT 6 – Pasatiempos

Glosarios

About the unit

In this first unit you will learn to ask and answer simple questions about yourself in Spanish. You will learn some useful classroom phrases and vocabulary for classroom objects as well as basic rules of pronunciation and spelling.

New contexts:

- meeting and greeting people, both formally and informally
- personal details (name, age, birthday)
- the alphabet
- months, dates, days of the week
- classroom objects
- classroom instructions

New language content:

- asking and responding to simple questions using *¿Cómo? ¿Cuándo? ¿Qué?* and *¿Cuánto?*
- introduction to verbs in first and second persons singular
- numbers 1–31
- rules and guidance for pronunciation and spelling
- definite and indefinite articles
- plurals of nouns
- hay and no hay

¡Hola y adiós!

Now then, as in all good language courses, we need first to learn how to say hello, good day, good afternoon/evening and good night. Listen carefully to the CD and try to imitate what you hear.

Note how in Spanish the exclamation mark is written upside down (¡) at the start of the phrase, and again the right way up at the end. The same happens with question marks (¿), as we will see. Notice also the accent on the *i* of *días*. For more on accents, see page 6.

¿Cómo te llamas?

Then, if we are feeling more chatty, we need to be able to introduce ourselves correctly.

Tú and usted

¿Cómo te llamas? ("what are you called?") is used to address young people or people you know well (the "familiar" form). *¿Cómo se llama **usted?*** also means "what are you called?", but is a more formal form of address, used when addressing adults or people you do not know well (the "polite" form).

¿Qué tal?

Then we should ask each other how we are...and say goodbye.

Exercise 1.1

¡Escucha y habla con tu amigo / amiga!
It is important when learning a language that you practise what you have learnt orally, i.e. **say** it out loud, as often as possible. So, listen to the examples and then, in pairs:

1. Greet your friend.
    Ask his/her name.
    Tell him/her what your name is.

    Ask him/her how he/she is.
    Tell him/her how you are.
    Say goodbye.

2. Then repeat this process, this time speaking to an adult. Remember to use the formal form with *usted* (i.e. *¿Cómo se llama usted?*)

Exercise 1.2

¡Lee y escribe!
It is also very important that you are able to **write** accurately in the language, paying careful attention to spelling. Copy the following phrases, and then translate them into English.

1. *¡Hola!*
2. *Buenos días. ¿Cómo te llamas?*
3. *Me llamo Elena.*
4. *¡Buenos días! Me llamo Jorge. ¿Qué tal?*
5. *Muy buenas. ¿Qué tal?*
6. *Bien, gracias.*
7. *Buenas tardes. ¿Cómo se llama usted?*
8. *Buenas tardes. Me llamo Carolina. ¿Cómo está usted?*
9. *Regular, gracias. ¿Qué tal?*
10. *Fenomenal, gracias. Adiós.*

Vocabulario

Adiós = goodbye	*Habla* = speak
Buenos días = good morning	*¡Hasta la vista!* = see you later
Buenas noches = good night	*¡Hasta luego!* = bye/see you later
Buenas tardes = good afternoon	*Hola* = hello
¿Cómo está usted? = how are you?	*Lee* = read
¿Cómo te llamas? = what is your name	*Me llamo* = my name is
Escribe = write	*Muy bien* = very well
Escucha = listen	*Muy buenas* = hi there
Fatal = awful	*¿Qué hay/tal?* = how are you doing?
Fenomenal = brilliant	*Regular* = not too bad, so so
Gracias = thankyou	*Tu amigo / amiga* = your friend
	Y = and

Exercise 1.3

¡Habla y escribe en español!

Best of all, as you're here to learn Spanish properly, you should be able to speak *and* write with equal fluency and accuracy. So we recommend that wherever you are asked to speak (*¡habla!*), you should also be able to write it down; and whenever you are asked to write something (*¡escribe!*), you should also be able to say it aloud. That way you will soon be more fluent in Spanish than a fluent thing.

N.B. the Spanish word for Spanish (*español*) begins with a small letter *e*. This is the same for all nationalities. All part of the fun!

Buenas tardes, amigo.

Buenas tardes, amiga.

You	**Your partner**
Good afternoon.	Good afternoon.
I am called —————. What is your name?	My name is —————.
How are you?	I am fine thank you. How are you?
Brilliant, thank you. Goodbye.	See you later.

Los números 1–12

The numbers in Spanish from 1 – 12 are very easy to recognise if you have met them in French (or Latin, for that matter). The spelling can be a bit awkward, though, so take care. The Spanish for zero, should you need it, is *cero*.

1.	Uno		7.	Siete
2.	Dos		8.	Ocho
3.	Tres		9.	Nueve
4.	Cuatro		10.	Diez
5.	Cinco		11.	Once
6.	Seis		12.	Doce

Exercise 1.4

¡Escucha, mira y escribe!

1. Listen to the CD and write down the numbers that you hear.
2. Look at the dice and give the total that you see.

Exercise 1.5

¡Habla!

Now say out loud the following numbers in Spanish. Then get your friend (or the dog) to say them out to you and see if you can write them down correctly.

1. 1 2 3 4 5 6 7 8 9 0
2. 0 1 2 3 3 4 4 5 5 6 6
3. 0 9 8 7 6 5 4 3 2 1
4. 0 2 4 6 8 8 0 0

5. 0 7 7 8 4 2 2 3 3 5
6. 0 7 7 7 5 3 1 5 6 9 8
7. 0 2 0 7 7 8 9 4 5 3 2
8. 0 2 2 5 6 3 6 9 7 4 1

Exercise 1.6

¡Habla y escribe!

And now for some maths….

1. *Dos + dos =*
2. *Cuatro + uno =*
3. *Cinco + seis =*
4. *Ocho + cuatro =*
5. *Seis + cuatro =*

6. *Diez – uno =*
7. *Nueve – cuatro =*
8. *Ocho + dos =*
9. *Doce – cuatro =*
10. *Diez – siete =*

Exercise 1.7

¡Escucha y escribe las respuestas!

Listen to the CD and give the answers to the sums put to the following pupils

1. *Elena*
2. *Teresa*
3. *Ester*
4. *Pedro*

> **Vocabulario**
> *Más* = plus (+)
> *Menos* = minus (-)
> *Son* = equals (=)

Exercise 1.8

¡Habla!

1. 3 + 5 = 8 **❮** *tres más cinco son ocho*
2. 2 + 1 =
3. 7 + 4 =
4. 5 – 3 =
5. 10 – 1 =

Exercise 1.9

Now for a game of Bingo. Listen to the CD and shout 'Bingo' when you get 3 numbers in a line.

El alfabeto

Now that we have learnt quite a lot of Spanish, we must have a quick look at the Spanish alphabet.

A B C **CH** D E F G
H I J K L **LL** M N
Ñ O P Q R S T U
V W X Y Z

It's not wildly exciting, and as you can see most of the letters are the same as ours. However notice the three funny chaps: **CH**, **LL** and **Ñ**. In most (but not all) dictionaries and vocabularies, these three letters are listed as separate entries.

- **CH** is pronounced as in the English word CHURCH. For example the word **ch**ile is pronounced as it is in English.
- **LL** is used to create the Y sound we get in the middle of the word MILLION. For example the word **ll**amo is pronounced **y**-amo.
- **Ñ** is used to make the sound ny as in the English word ONION. For example the word **España** is pronounced espa**n-y**a.

Also note that the letter *W*, which is almost never used, is sometimes pronounced as a V.
Apart from that, the Spanish alphabet is perfectly normal.

Los acentos

The other little pit-fall to skirt around is the fact that Spanish uses accents to help you stress a word correctly. If you see an accent on a syllable, stress that syllable. For words with no accents, listen carefully to how they are pronounced. A broad rule of thumb is given below:

1. Generally the stress falls on the **penultimate** (i.e. the last but one) syllable of a Spanish word if the word ends in a vowel, *s* or *n*, or on the **final** syllable in the vast majority of other cases.
2. However, where this is *not* the case, an accent is placed to show us where to stress the word. For example the word *Adiós* is stressed on the final syllable, despite the fact that it ends in *s*. To let us know, they very kindly place an accent on the *o*.
3. A letter with an accent is said to be **con acento**. E.g. *é = e con acento*.

Exercise 1.10

¡Escucha y deletrea!
Listen to the CD. Try to get used to the sounds of the letters in Spanish and the way they fit together into words. Spell (*deletrea*) the words back to your partner and see if he/she can write them down correctly.

1. *España*
2. *Barcelona*
3. *Madrid*
4. *Inglaterra*
5. *Torremolinos*
6. *Costa Brava*
7. *Granada*
8. *Sevilla*
9. *Chile*
10. *Benidorm*

Exercise 1.11

¡Escucha y escribe!
1. Listen to the CD and complete the following table:

Francisco	vive en	Sevilla
E......................	vive en	....
R......................	vive en	....
Ed....................	vive en	....
C......................	vive en	....

"Vamos a pasar lista."

2. Listen carefully to the CD, and then write down the Spanish names that you hear in order as the teacher takes the register. Don't forget that, to say that a vowel has an accent on it, one says it is **con acento.**

Exercise 1.12

¡Habla!
Deletrea tu nombre.

Pronunciation

Now that you have heard quite a lot of Spanish being spoken, let's take a closer look at the way Spanish is pronounced. Here are some rules which will help:
1. Never pronounce the letter **H**. E.g. *¡Habla!* sounds like *'abla'.*
2. The letter **C** followed by *E* or *I* is pronounced TH as in "thistle". E.g. *on**ce**, die**ci**séis.*
3. The letter **G** followed by *E* or *I* is pronounced rather like the rough noise we hear in the Scottish word loch. E.g. **Ge**ografía, **Gi**braltar.
4. The letter **J** makes a sound which is very similar to the rough G sound above. E.g. *Jesús.*
5. The letter **Z** is pronounced TH as in "thistle". E.g. *Cádiz.*
6. The letters **B** and **V** are pronounced in exactly the same way, both making a noise like the B in the word "baby". E.g. **baca** = roof-rack and **vaca** = cow are pronounced the same!
7. The letter **R** at the start of a word is lightly trilled (rolled). E.g. **R**amón, **R**oberto.
8. **RR** is always strongly trilled. E.g. *Torremolinos.*
9. **Qu** is pronounced like the letter **k**. E.g. **Qu**ince.

Exercise 1.13

Study the rules for pronunciation above. Then, using the words given below, link each word to one of the rules. Say each word out loud. Then, using the vocabulary at the back of the book, see if you can find further examples of Spanish words which illustrate each rule.

1.	Habitante	11.	Galaxia	21.	Bonito
2.	Helicóptero	12.	General	22.	Barato
3.	Inhumano	13.	Gimnasia	23.	Vaso
4.	Calibre	14.	Gibraltareño	24.	Vídeo
5.	Correcto	15.	Jabón	25.	Viejo
6.	Curiosidad	16.	Jarra	26.	Respuesta
7.	Centroamérica	17.	Zoo	27.	Regresar
8.	César	18.	Zanzibar	28.	Arriba
9.	Cine	19.	Zaragoza	29.	Inglaterra
10.	Cigarrillo	20.	Baño	30.	Querer

¿Cuántos años tienes?

We have already met the numbers from 1-12. Assuming that you are now, or hope one day to be, older than twelve years old, we need some more numbers before we can begin to tell our ages. If you are older than thirty-one, tough! You will just have to wait! By the way, while we're at it, look how similar these numbers are in French...

	español		francés	
13	Trece		Treize	
14	Catorce		Quatorze	
15	Quince		Quinze	
16	Dieciséis		Seize	
17	Diecisiete		Dix-sept	
18	Dieciocho		Dix-huit	
19	Diecinueve		Dix-neuf	
20	Veinte		Vingt	
21	Veintiuno		Vingt et un	
22	Veintidós		Vingt-deux	
23	Veintitrés		Vingt-trois	
24	Veinticuatro		Vingt-quatre	
25	Veinticinco		Vingt-cinq	
26	Veintiséis		Vingt-six	
27	Veintisiete		Vingt-sept	
28	Veintiocho		Vingt-huit	
29	Veintinueve		Vingt-neuf	
30	Treinta		Trente	
31	Treinta y uno		Trente et un	

E.g. *¿Cuántos años tienes?* = How old are you? (literally = How many years do you have?)
Tengo once años = I am eleven years old (literally = I have eleven years).
E.g. *¿Cuántos años tiene el profesor?* = How old is the teacher?
El profesor tiene veintidós años = the teacher is twenty-two years old.

Note
Tengo, tienes and *tiene* all come from the verb *tener* = to have. We will have fun with verbs later in Unit 2.

Exercise 1.14

¡Habla!
In pairs, ask your partner how old he/she is and then say how old you are.

Exercise 1.15

¡Lee!
More maths! Match up the questions (1-5) to the correct answers (A-E).
1. *Tengo quince más dos.*
2. *Tengo trece más seis.*
3. *Tengo doce más once.*
4. *Tengo veintidós menos catorce.*
5. *Tengo treinta y uno menos veinticinco.*

A. *Tengo ocho.*
B. *Tengo veintitrés.*
C. *Tengo diecisiete.*
D. *Tengo seis.*
E. *Tengo diecinueve.*

Exercise 1.16

¡Escucha y escribe las respuestas!

Número 1	*Número 5*
Número 2	*Número 6*
Número 3	*Número 7*
Número 4	*Número 8*

> **Vocabulario**
> *Multiplicado por* = multiplied by
> *Dividido por* = divided by
> *La respuesta* = the answer
> *La ficha* = the table
> *Rellena* = fill in

Exercise 1.17

¡Escucha y rellena la ficha!
¿Cuántos años tienen? Take care with the last two!

José	José tiene 11 años.
María	María tiene ....
Jesús	....
Juan	....
Teresa	....
Miguel y Rafael	....
Carmen (¡!)	....
Pedro (¡!)	....

> **¡N.B.!**
> *Tendrá* = **FUTURE** tense, i.e. (he)
>   will be
> *El año que viene* = next year
> *Mañana* = tomorrow

Exercise 1.18

¡Lee y escucha!
Learning your numbers should be like learning your tables in maths. They need to be absolutely drilled into your brain. Which numbers have been left out of the following sequences? If you know your numbers properly it should be obvious immediately (as it would be if we did this in English).

1.   *Once, doce, trece, quince*
2.   *Veinticuatro, veintiséis, veintisiete, veintiocho*
3.   *Trece, catorce, dieciséis, diecisiete*
4.   *Seis, ocho, nueve, diez*
5.   *Veintisiete, veintiocho, treinta, treinta y uno*
6.   *Diecinueve, veintiuno, veintidós, veintitrés*

Exercise 1.19

¡Escucha!
Bingo
Who wins the bingo – José, Rafael or Carolina? Copy the three cards. Then cross off the numbers as you hear them and shout BINGO when one of the three cards is complete.

5	9	1	17
20	7	8	14
11	21	3	10
30	22	7	28

José's card

1	8	5	4
19	7	11	10
6	16	9	20
18	17	31	29

Rafael's card

3	5	20	28
2	13	1	10
9	11	15	18
14	22	27	19

Carolina's card

Los meses y las estaciones del año

And now for the months and seasons of the year. Note that these only begin with a capital letter if they come at the start of a sentence.

```
           enero                    febrero                   marzo                    abril
lu      4  11  18  25        lu  1   8  15  22        lu  1   8  15  22  29     lu      5  12  19  26
ma      5  12  19  26        ma  2   9  16  23        ma  2   9  16  23  30     ma      6  13  20  27
mi      6  13  20  27        mi  3  10  17  24        mi  3  10  17  24  31     mi      7  14  21  28
ju      7  14  21  28        ju  4  11  18  25        ju  4  11  18  25         ju  1   8  15  22  29
vi  1   8  15  22  29        vi  5  12  19  26        vi  5  12  19  26         vi  2   9  16  23  30
sa  2   9  16  23  30        sa  6  13  20  27        sa  6  13  20  27         sa  3  10  17  24
do  3  10  17  24  31        do  7  14  21  28        do  7  14  21  28         do  4  11  18  25

           mayo                     junio                     julio                    agosto
lu      3  10  17  24  31    lu      7  14  21  28    lu      5  12  19  26     lu      2   9  16  23  30
ma      4  11  18  25        ma  1   8  15  22  29    ma      6  13  20  27     ma      3  10  17  24  31
mi      5  12  19  26        mi  2   9  16  23  30    mi      7  14  21  28     mi      4  11  18  25
ju      6  13  20  27        ju  3  10  17  24        ju  1   8  15  22  29     ju      5  12  19  26
vi      7  14  21  28        vi  4  11  18  25        vi  2   9  16  23  30     vi      6  13  20  27
sa  1   8  15  22  29        sa  5  12  19  26        sa  3  10  17  24  31     sa      7  14  21  28
do  2   9  16  23  30        do  6  13  20  27        do  4  11  18  25         do  1   8  15  22  29

         septiembre                 octubre                   noviembre                diciembre
lu      6  13  20  27        lu      4  11  18  25    lu  1   8  15  22  29     lu      6  13  20  27
ma      7  14  21  28        ma      5  12  19  26    ma  2   9  16  23  30     ma      7  14  21  28
mi  1   8  15  22  29        mi      6  13  20  27    mi  3  10  17  24         mi  1   8  15  22  29
ju  2   9  16  23  30        ju      7  14  21  28    ju  4  11  18  25         ju  2   9  16  23  30
vi  3  10  17  24            vi  1   8  15  22  29    vi  5  12  19  26         vi  3  10  17  24  31
sa  4  11  18  25            sa  2   9  16  23  30    sa  6  13  20  27         sa  4  11  18  25
do  5  12  19  26            do  3  10  17  24  31    do  7  14  21  28         do  5  12  19  26
```

Las estaciones = the seasons
La primavera = spring
El verano = summer

Los meses = the months
El otoño = autumn
El invierno = winter

La Fecha

Note that the formula for giving a date in Spanish is very simple:
E.g. *El 1 de enero* = 1st January.
E.g. *El 12 de octubre* = 12th October.

Notice also the formula *del 2 al 3 de abril* = from the 2nd to the 3rd of April.

Exercise 1.20

¡Escucha y rellena la ficha!
Listen to the CD, which gives details of some Spanish festivals (*las fiestas*). Then copy and complete the table of dates below.

Fiesta	Fecha
El día de la Hispanidad	El 12 de octubre
Las fallas de Valencia	
San Isidro	
Todos los Santos	
San Juan	
La Tomatina	
La Tamborrada	
Navidad	
El día de Reyes	
San Fermín	
Las Nieves Pontevedra	
Feria de abril	

Exercise 1.21

¡Habla!

A Spanish teenager is visiting the UK and wants to know about various key dates in the UK. Give the dates of the following (you may need to look some of these up yourself!):

1.	Christmas Eve	7.	St. Valentines Day
2.	Christmas Day	8.	St. George's Day
3.	Boxing Day	9.	St. Andrew's Day
4.	New Year's Eve	10.	St. Patrick's Day
5.	New Year's Day	11.	St. David's Day
6.	Your birthday	12.	Midsummer's Day

¿Cuándo es tu cumpleaños?

Now that we can count to 31 and we know the months of the year, we can ask people the date of their birthday (*el cumpleaños*).

¿Cuándo es tu cumpleaños? (familiar form)
Mi cumpleaños es el 15 de octubre.
¿Cuándo es su cumpleaños? (polite form)
Mi cumpleaños es el 23 de julio.

Note this use of *su* when addressing someone using the polite form (more on this in Unit 2). We can also use it to ask when someone else's birthday is:
¿Cuándo es el cumpleaños de Lucy?
Su cumpleaños es el 7 de abril.

> **Vocabulario**
> *Mi* = my
> *Tu* = your
> *Su* = his, her (or it can mean "your" when we are using the polite form of address)

Exercise 1.22

¡Habla!

Take turns to ask when your friends' birthdays are and how old they are. Then reply.

E.g. *¿Cuándo es tu cumpleaños y cuántos años tienes?*
     Mi cumpleaños es el 27 de noviembre y tengo quince años.

Don't forget, if you are addressing an adult in the polite form, this will become :
¿Cuándo es su cumpleaños y cuántos años tiene?

Exercise 1.23

¡Escucha!
¿Cuándo es su cumpleaños?
1. *Manuel*
2. *Severiano*
3. *Juan*
4. *José*
5. *Pepe*
6. *Carolina*

Exercise 1.24

¡Escucha!
¿Cuántos años tiene?
1. *Manuel*
2. *Severiano*
3. *Juan*
4. *José*
5. *Pepe*
6. *Carolina*

Exercise 1.25

¡Escucha y rellena la ficha!
Listen carefully to the CD and then, for each character, give their name, city, age and birthday.

Nombre	Ciudad	Edad	Cumpleaños
1. María	Barcelona	15 años	22 febrero
2.	Toledo	....	....
3.	....	....	12 marzo
4.	....	18	....
5. Miguel	....	....	....

Los días de la semana

Monday	*lunes*
Tuesday	*martes*
Wednesday	*miércoles*
Thursday	*jueves*
Friday	*viernes*
Saturday	*sábado*
Sunday	*domingo*

N.B. The days of the week are written with a small letter, the same as the months and seasons.

Exercise 1.26

¡Habla!
Practise asking your partner the following questions.

1. *¿Qué fecha es hoy?*
2. *Es el....*
3. *¿Qué día es hoy?*
4. *Es...*
5. *¿Y mañana?*
6. *Mañana es...*
7. *¿Y ayer?*
8. *Ayer fue...*
9. *¿Cuál es tu día favorito?*
10. *Es...*

Conversation

You have now learnt enough Spanish to have a simple conversation. The key to success here is to listen carefully to Spanish when it is being spoken, and to concentrate on speaking as accurately as you can. Think how horrid it sounds when someone speaks to you in very bad English, so be sure not to put your Spanish friends through this ordeal. A quick squint at the vocabulary on the next page could prove helpful.

Exercise 1.27

¡Habla!
Use the following pictures as a prompt for a simple conversation between you and your partner.

Vocabulario

Learning vocabulary is not the most exciting activity dreamed up for mankind, but it has to be done, so we suggest you make it a regular part of your studies. That way you can keep on top of it and won't go into a blind sweat when an exam looms on the horizon, or you get the call-up to go to Spain. Break it up into topics, and you'll be fine. In this book there are twelve vocabularies (numbered 1.1 to 6.2, two per unit) which we suggest you pay particular attention to. They include the words covered so far which you really need to learn by heart. Good luck!

Vocabulario 1.1

Hola = hi, hello
Adiós = goodbye
Buenas noches = good night
Buenas tardes = good afternoon/evening
Buenos días = good day/morning
Hasta la vista = see you later
Hasta luego = bye/see you later

¿Cómo te llamas? = what are you called? (informal form)
¿Cómo se llama usted? = what are you called? (formal form)
Me llamo = I am called

¿Qué hay? = how are you doing?
¿Qué tal? = how are you?
Bien = well
Regular = not too bad, so so
Fatal = awful
Fenomenal = brilliant
Muy bien = very well
Muy buenas = hi there
Gracias = thanks

¿Cuál? = which?
¿Cuántos? = how many?
¿Cuándo? = when?
¿Qué? = what?

Tengo = I have
Tienes = you have
Tiene = he / she has

Y = and
De = of
Con = with

El número = the number
El teléfono = the telephone
El alfabeto = the alphabet
El nombre = the name
El acento = the accent
La ciudad = the city
La edad = the age

El día = the day
El año = the year
La semana = the week
El cumpleaños = the birthday
La fecha = the date
La estación = the season
El mes = the month

Hoy = today
Mañana = tomorrow
Ayer = yesterday

Más = plus
Menos = minus
Son = equals (literally = *are*)
Multiplicado por = multiplied by
Dividido por = divided by

¡Deletrea! = spell!
¡Escribe! = write!
¡Escucha! = listen!
¡Habla! = speak!
¡Lee! = read!
¡Mira! = look at!
¡Rellena! = fill in!
El profesor / la profesora = the teacher
El amigo / la amiga = the friend
La respuesta = the answer
La ficha = the form, chart

As you will have noticed, some Spanish words use *el* for "the" and some use *la*; some use *los* and some use *las*. Turn the page, and you'll see why...

La clase

Here are some things that you might expect to find in a typical classroom.

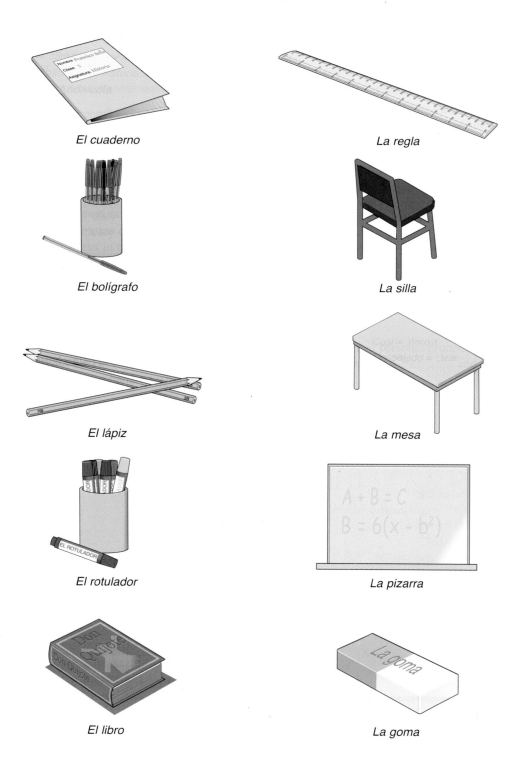

El cuaderno

La regla

El bolígrafo

La silla

El lápiz

La mesa

El rotulador

La pizarra

El libro

La goma

Nouns and gender

It goes without saying that a man in Spanish is masculine and a woman is feminine. Similarly, a boy is masculine and a girl is feminine. The big difference is that all *things* in Spanish (e.g. planks, computers, biscuits etc.) are either masculine or feminine! However there are some general rules of thumb for working out which gender the various things are, so it's not all doom and gloom.

- The vast majority of words which end in *-o* are masculine.
- The vast majority of words which end in *-a* are feminine.
- All words that end in *-dad* or *-ción* are feminine.

In this book we shall use **blue for masculine** and **red for feminine** whenever we feel you may need a little extra help.

Vocabulario

Bolígrafo, el	= the pen	*Goma, la*	= the rubber
Cuaderno, el	= the exercise book	*Mesa, la*	= the table
Libro, el	= the book	*Pared, la*	= the wall
Lápiz, el	= the pencil	*Pizarra, la*	= the whiteboard
Rotulador, el	= the board-marker	*Regla, la*	= the ruler
Sacapuntas, el	= the pencil-sharpener	*Silla, la*	= the chair

Definite article

Spanish has different words for "**the**" depending on whether the noun is masculine or feminine, singular or plural:

	Singular	**Plural**
Masculine	*El chico* = the boy	*Los chicos* = the boys
Feminine	*La chica* = the girl	*Las chicas* = the girls

Indefinite article

The same is true of the indefinite article, the word for "**a**":

	Singular	**Plural**
Masculine	*Un chico* = a boy	*Unos chicos* = some boys
Feminine	*Una chica* = a girl	*Unas chicas* = some girls

Exercise 1.28

¡Habla con tu amigo!

Now practise your wonderful Spanish accent and grasp of vocabulary by looking around for each of the items you have learnt above. For this it will help if you know two little phrases: *¿dónde está?* = where is? and *aquí está* = here is.

E.g. *¿Dónde está el cuaderno?* = Where is the exercise book?

   Aquí está el cuaderno = Here is the exercise book.

Exercise 1.29

¡Lee y escucha! Escribe en inglés.
Read the following text and then translate it into English:

¿Dónde está mi libro?

Buenos días, José.
Buenos días, Rosa.
¿Dónde está el bolígrafo?
Aquí está el bolígrafo.
¿Dónde está el libro?
Aquí está el libro.
¿Dónde está el rotulador?
Aquí está, en la mesa.

N.B.
En means "in" or "on".

Exercise 1.30

¡Habla con tu pareja!
Using the pictures below as a guide, have a conversation with your partner (*tu pareja*), making use of the words and phrases you have met so far. You may need to look up some words in the vocabulary at the back of the book.

Singular and plural

Now we need to learn how to make nouns plural. Well it's pretty straightforward, actually. Think of English: one book, two book**s**, one potato, two potato**es.** We simply add the letter s, or sometimes –es. Exactly the same happens in Spanish. The rule is:

- if the noun ends in a vowel, add **s**;
- if the noun ends in a consonant, add **es**.

Singular		**Plural**	
Un bolígrafo	A pen	*Unos bolígrafo***S**	Some pens
Una mesa	A table	*Unas mesa***S**	Some tables
Un rotulador	A marker	*Unos rotulador***es**	Some markers
Una pared	A wall	*Unas pared***es**	Some walls

Note

Words ending in *z* change the *z* to *c* before adding *es*. For example the plural of *un lápiz* (= a pencil) is *unos lápices*.

Exercise 1.31

¡Escribe en español!
Here's a quick exercise to see if you have understood. Give the Spanish for:

1. A book
2. Some books
3. A table
4. Some tables
5. The exercise book
6. The exercise books
7. A rubber
8. The rubbers
9. A chair
10. Some chairs

Exercise 1.32

¡Habla y escribe!
Again, give the Spanish for what you see in the pictures. Remember, if you see more than one of a particular object, make it plural.

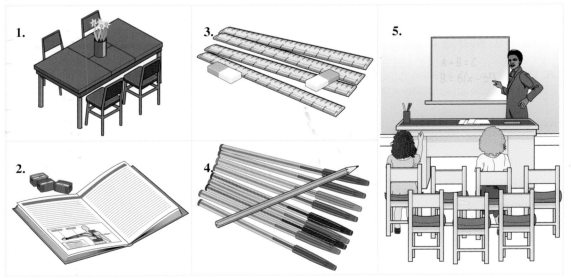

1.
2.
3.
4.
5.

Exercise 1.33

¡Escribe!
Put the following into the plural. Then translate:
1. *El año*
2. *Un chico*
3. *La clase*
4. *Un acento*
5. *El número*
6. *Una silla*
7. *La profesora*
8. *Una mesa*
9. *El nombre*
10. *La regla*

"Por favor, profesor.
¿Tiene usted
un lápiz?"

Por favor

If you need to ask for something, don't forget to use *por favor* = please.
E.g. *¿Tienes un lápiz, por favor?* or *¿Por favor, tienes un lápiz?*
     Do you have a pencil, please?

Remember, if you are asking your teacher you should use the polite form with *usted*.
E.g. *Por favor, profesor. ¿Tiene usted un lápiz?*

Exercise 1.34

¡Escucha!
¿Verdad o mentira? Escucha y escribe verdad (✓) o mentira (✗), como en el ejemplo.
1. *José tiene un rotulador.* ✓
2. *José no tiene una regla.*
3. *Miguel tiene un libro de español.*
4. *Miguel no tiene un cuaderno.*
5. *Ana tiene un bolígrafo.*
6. *Ana no tiene una goma.*
7. *María tiene un lápiz.*
8. *María no tiene un sacapuntas.*

Vocabulario	
Sí = yes	*Verdad* = true
No = no, not	*Mentira* = false
De nada = not at all	*O* = or
Lo siento = I'm sorry	

N.B. The negative in Spanish is very easy; simply put *no* in front of the verb.
E.g. *José no tiene un rotulador* = José does not have a marker.

Exercise 1.35

¡Habla!
In pairs, ask each other whether you have various objects and reply, as in the example.

¡Hola, Miguel! ¿Tienes un libro?
No, no tengo un libro.

Exercise. 1.36

¡Lee y escucha!

Profesora:	Buenos días, chicos.
Alumnos:	Buenos días, señorita.
Profesora:	José, ¿qué tienes en tu mochila? ¿Tienes tus libros?
José:	Sí, señorita. Tengo tres libros en mi mochila. Tengo mi libro de español, mi libro de inglés y mi cuaderno.
Profesora:	Bien. Y tú, Teresa, ¿tienes tus libros?
Teresa:	Sí. Pero no tengo mi libro de historia.
Profesora:	¿Dónde está?
Teresa:	Está en casa. Está en la mesa en casa. Lo siento.
Profesora:	No importa. Eduardo, ¿tienes tus libros?
Eduardo:	No, señorita. Mis libros están en casa.
Profesora:	¿Tienes tu bolígrafo?
Eduardo:	¡No, mi bolígrafo está en el autobús!
Profesora:	No tienes tus libros ni tu bolígrafo, pero tienes tu regla, ¿verdad?
Eduardo:	No, señorita. Creo que Teresa tiene mi regla.
Teresa:	¡Qué va! No tengo su regla.
Eduardo:	¡Qué sí!
Teresa:	¡Qué no! Eduardo es imbécil!
Profesora:	¡Oye! ¡Basta! Eduardo, ¿tienes tu calculadora?
Eduardo:	Sí, claro.
Profesora:	¿Dónde está tu calculadora?
Eduardo:	Está en mi mochila, claro.
Profesora:	¿Estás seguro?
Eduardo:	Sí, aquí está ... ¡Ay! no tengo mi calculadora. Quizás Teresa ...
Teresa:	¡Qué va! Eduardo es ....
Profesora:	¡Basta!

Vocabulario

La mochila = the school-bag

Inglés = English

Pero = but
¿Dónde está? = where is (it)?

No importa = never mind

El autobús = the bus
Ni = nor

Creo que = I think that
¡Qué va! = no way!

Imbécil = stupid
¡Basta! = enough!
La calculadora = the calculator

Claro = of course
Seguro = sure

Quizás = perhaps

A. ¡Escribe!

Rellena los huecos y escribe en inglés, como en el ejemplo:

José tiene ....*tres*.... libros en su mochila.

José has three books in his school-bag.

1. Teresa no tiene su ....
2. Su libro de historia está .... en casa.
3. El bolígrafo de Eduardo está................................
4. Eduardo no tiene sus ...., ni su .... ni su..............ni su...............
5. Eduardo cree que ....tiene su calculadora.

B. ¡Habla!

Practica un diálogo con tu pareja, como en el ejemplo:

"¿Tienes un cuaderno en tu mochila?"
"Sí, tengo dos cuadernos."

"¿Tienes una regla en tu mochila?"
"No, no tengo ninguna regla."

¿Qué es esto?

A useful way of increasing your vocabulary in Spanish is to ask your teacher the simple question *¿qué es esto?* = what is this? Do this whenever you wish to know the Spanish for something that you can see around you.

Exercise 1.37

¡Habla!
¿Qué es esto?
Ask someone, and then check these words in the vocabulary at the back of the book.

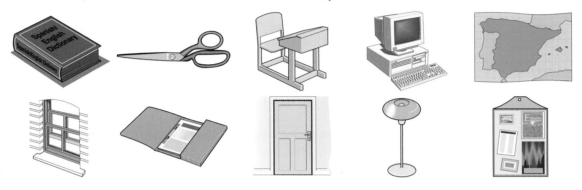

En mi mochila tengo...

Another useful trick for building vocabulary is to play memory games. For example you can play a version of the game "I packed my Saratoga trunk and in it I put..."
E.g.   *En mi mochila tengo un lápiz.*
        En mi mochila tengo un lápiz y una regla.
        En mi mochila tengo un lápiz, una regla y tres libros.

Hay

A useful little word to know at this stage is *hay*, meaning both there is and there are.

E.g.   *¿Qué hay en tu mochila?*
        Hay un lápiz en mi mochila.
E.g.   *¿Qué hay en tu mochila?*
        Hay tres libros en mi mochila

Exercise 1.38

¡Habla!
¿Qué hay en tu mochila?
In pairs, tell each other what you have or do not have in your school bag. If your bag happens to be empty, the following phrases might be useful:
No tengo nada = I do not have anything.
No hay nada = there is not anything.

Los imperativos

To give an order in Spanish we need to use a form of the verb called the imperative. We will learn about verbs properly later, but for now we will make do with some common forms which you can use around the classroom. The two forms given here are the singular and plural forms. When giving an order to one person only, use the first (singular) form; when giving an order to more than one person, use the second (plural) form.

Escucha / escuchad = listen
Mira / mirad = look at
Saca / Sacad = take out
Trabaja / trabajad = work
Escribe / escribid = write
Siéntate / sentaos = sit down
Levántate / levantaos = get up
Cállate / callaos = be quiet

Un juego = a game

¡Escucha!
Listen to the instructions on the CD but remember, only do what Simon says!

¿Cómo se dice en español?

Now for some more practice at working out vocabulary. Whatever stage you are at, there will always be more words you need to learn. If the person you are talking to speaks English, a useful way of increasing your Spanish vocabulary is to ask: *¿cómo se dice en español?* = How does one say in Spanish?

E.g. *¿Cómo se dice en español* "the house"?
En español se dice "la casa".

This might lead to questions such as:

¿Cómo se escribe "casa"?
En español se escribe "casa": c-a-s-a; or

¿Cómo se pronuncia "c-a-s-a"?
Se pronuncia casa.

Exercise 1.39

¡Habla!
In pairs, look about you for objects and ask the three questions:
¿Cómo se dice en español?
¿Cómo se pronuncia?
*¿Cómo se escribe?**

*Alternatively, you might just use the phrase *¡deletrea la palabra!* (spell the word!).

Exercise 1.40

¡Escucha!
Write down the objects, correctly spelled, chosen by the following pupils:
1. *José*
2. *María*
3. *David*
4. *Ana*

Exercise 1.41

¡Lee o escucha y contesta las preguntas!

En el colegio

Hoy es martes, quince de noviembre. Hay treinta alumnos en la clase. Hay dieciocho chicos y doce chicas. El profesor se llama Roberto Pérez. Tiene treinta años. Su cumpleaños es el uno de noviembre – el día de Todos los Santos. Una alumna se llama Carolina – tiene quince años. Tiene una mochila. Hay cinco libros en su mochila. Un alumno se llama José pero no tiene nada en su mochila.

1.   *¿Qué día es hoy?*
2.   *¿Cuántos alumnos hay en la clase?*
3.   *¿Cuántos chicos hay?*
4.   *¿Cómo se llama el profesor?*
5.   *¿Cuántos años tiene?*
6.   *¿Cuándo es su cumpleaños?*
7.   *¿Qué hay en la mochila de Carolina?*
8.   *¿Cómo se llama el alumno que no tiene nada en su mochila?*

Exercise 1.42

¡Habla!

With your partner, prepare a conversation using as much as possible of the Spanish vocabulary that you have learnt so far. If possible, record your efforts, or better still film them, and play the result back to the class.

Entrevistas

A common form of torture for people learning a new language is to make them conduct interviews (*entrevistas*) on one another. Here then is some practice at this, first using the familiar form and then using the polite form.

1.   *Entrevista a un amigo / una amiga* (familiar form)
      ¡Lee y escucha!

Tú:	*¿Cómo te llamas?*
Amigo/a:	*Me llamo Ángel Hernández.*
Tú:	*¿Cuántos años tienes?*
Amigo/a:	*Tengo dieciséis años.*
Tú:	*¿Cuándo es tu cumpleaños?*
Amigo/a:	*Es el quince de marzo.*
Tú:	*¿Cómo se escribe tu nombre?*
Amigo/a:	*A con acento N-G-E-L*
Tú:	*¿Y Hernández?*
Amigo/a:	*H-E-R-N-A con acento – N-D-E-Z*

2. *Entrevista a un profesor* (polite form)
   ¡Lee y escucha!

Tú:	*¿Cómo se llama usted?*
Profesor:	*Me llamo Esteban Martínez.*
Tú:	*¿Cómo se escribe Martínez?*
Profesor:	*M-A-R-T-I con acento– N-E-Z*
Tú:	*¿Cuántos años tiene usted?*
Profesor:	*Tengo treinta y nueve años.*
Tú:	*¿Cuándo es su cumpleaños?*
Profesor:	*Es el dos de mayo.*

Vocabulario 1.2

Alumno(a), el (la)	= the student	*Pared, la*	= the wall
Bolígrafo, el	= the pen	*Pizarra, la*	= the whiteboard
Chico, el	= the boy	*Regla, la*	= the ruler
Cuaderno, el	= the exercise book	*Silla, la*	= the chair
Diccionario, el	= the dictionary	*Tijeras, las*	= the scissors
Estuche, el	= the pencil-case	*Ventana, la*	= the window
Lápiz, el	= the pencil		
Libro, el	= the book	*Claro*	= of course
Mapa, el	= the map	*Creo que*	= I think that
Ordenador, el	= the computer	*Lo siento*	= I'm sorry
Papel, el	= the paper	*No importa*	= never mind
Pupitre, el	= the desk	*Quizás*	= perhaps
Rotulador, el	= the board-marker	*Seguro*	= sure
Sacapuntas, el	= the pencil-sharpener		
Tablón, el	= the notice-board	*Aquí*	= here
Calculadora, la	= the calculator	*¿Cómo?*	= how
Carpeta, la	= the file	*¿Dónde?*	= where
Casa, la	= the home		
Chica, la	= the girl	*Mentira*	= lie
Clase, la	= the class	*Verdad*	= truth
Goma, la	= the rubber	*En*	= in, on
Mesa, la	= the table	*No*	= no, not
Mochila, la	= the school-bag	*O*	= or
Palabra, la	= the word	*Pero*	= but
		Sí	= yes

Deberes (= homework)
1. Prepare interviews with at least four of your friends, using the format of the familiar form interview opposite.
2. Research a famous personality from a Spanish-speaking country. With your partner, prepare an interview similar to the one above. **N.B.** in this case, remember to use the polite form (with *usted*)!

Summary of unit

At the end of this unit

You should now be able to: understand basic classroom instructions spoken by the teacher; greet people formally and informally; carry out short presentations about yourself using *y* and *pero*; hold simple conversations asking for information about others and giving information about yourself; identify and ask for classroom objects with the correct definite or indefinite article; make positive or negative responses to a request for an object; spell words, and ask for the meaning of the words you do not understand; use a dictionary to find the meaning or gender of a word you do not know; pronounce words that follow a regular pattern.

You might also be able to: say and write longer passages from memory; use some classroom expressions independently and ask for help in Spanish.

About the unit

In this unit you will learn to talk and write about your family, friends and pets, and how to describe your appearance.

New contexts:

- other people
- descriptions of family, friends, pets
- nationalities
- Christmas, fiestas

New language content:

- regular *-AR*, *-ER* and *-IR* verbs
- possessive adjectives
- asking questions with *¿Cómo? ¿Cuánto?* and *¿Quién?*
- irregular verbs *tener* and *ser* (all persons)
- agreement of adjectives
- intensifiers (*muy, bastante*)
- numbers 1–100

La familia

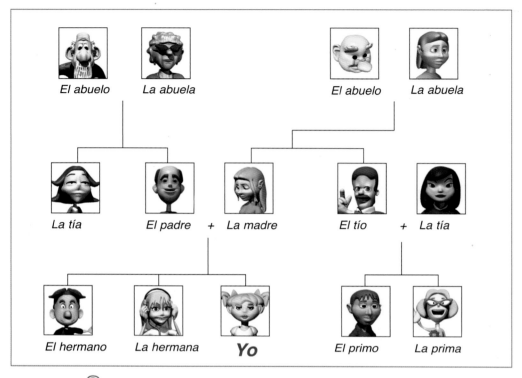

Exercise 2.1

¡Escucha y para cada persona contesta las preguntas, como en el ejemplo!

Listen to the descriptions and then, for each character, lay out the answers to the questions that follow in the table, as in the example:

Nombre	Edad	Personas en su familia	Hermanos	Hermanas	Cumpleaños
1. Laura	14	5	0	2	13 May
2.					
3.					
4.					
5.					
6.					

Vocabulario

El abuelo	= the grandfather	La abuela	= the grandmother
El padre	= the father	La madre	= the mother
El hermano	= the brother	La hermana	= the sister
El tío	= the uncle	La tía	= the aunt
El primo	= the cousin (masculine)	La prima	= the cousin (feminine)
El padrastro	= the step-father	La madrastra	= the step-mother
El hermanastro	= the step/half-brother	La hermanastra	= the step/half-sister
¿Cuántos?	= how many? (masculine)	¿Cuántas?	= how many (feminine)

Reflexive pronouns: a brief glimpse

In the last unit we learnt to say: *me llamo* = I am called, and *te llamas* = you are called. Now we are going to use *se llama* = he/she/it is called. In doing all of this, we are using reflexive pronouns (*me* = myself, *te* = yourself, *se* = himself/herself/itself). What we are actually saying is I call myself, you call yourself, he calls himself, etc. We will leave the plural forms of these until later, but in the meantime, don't ever say we keep things from you if they look hard!

Ejemplos: *¿Cómo se llama tu madre?*
Mi madre se llama Isabel.
¿Cómo se llama tu hermano?
Mi hermano se llama Jorge.

Possessive adjectives

The words for "my", "your", "his" etc. are possessive adjectives. Nothing to panic about except that, being adjectives, they change when used with plural nouns. You will learn more about adjectives on page 39.

E.g. **Mi** *amigo es de Madrid* = **my** friend is from Madrid.

E.g. **Mis** *amigos son de Barcelona* = **my** friends are from Barcelona.

Singular	Plural	
Mi	*mis*	my
Tu	*tus*	your
Su	*sus*	his or her or its or their

Points to note
1. **Su** means his, her, its and their.
E.g. *Su madre* = his mother OR her mother OR their mother.
2. As we saw in Unit 1, *su* is also used in the polite form to mean "your".
E.g. *¿Cómo se llama su madre, señor?* = What is your mother called, sir?

Exercise 2.2 ✍️

¡Escribe en inglés!
1. *Se llama Roberto.*
2. *Me llamo Raúl.*
3. *Mi hermana se llama Elena.*
4. *Tú te llamas Ana.*
5. *Mi amigo se llama José.*
6. *Usted se llama Antonio.*

Exercise: 2.3 💬

¡Habla!
With a partner, ask and answer questions such as the following:
1. *¿Cómo se llama tu hermano?*
2. *¿Cómo se llama tu madre?*
3. *¿Cómo se llama tu hermana?*
4. *¿Cómo se llama tu abuelo?*
5. *¿Cómo se llama tu tía?*
6. *¿Cómo se llama tu primo?*

In each case, you might like to add *¿Cómo se escribe?*

If you don't have any brothers or sisters, you may need this expression:
soy hijo único = I am an only child (if you are a boy); or
soy hija única (if you are a girl).

Exercise 2.4

¡Lee!

Using the following information, fill in the family-tree below.

Elena es la mujer de Carlos y la hermana de Pedro.
Carlos es el padre de David.
Juan es el hermano de David.
José es el nieto de Carlos.
Montse es la nieta de Carlos.
David es el tío de Montse.
Montse es la mujer de Jesús

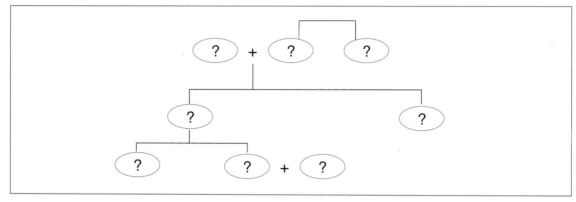

Exercise 2.5

¡Habla y escribe!

Say as much as you can about the following family tree:

E.g. *Carlos es el marido de Maribel. Es el padre de David y el abuelo de Antonio.*

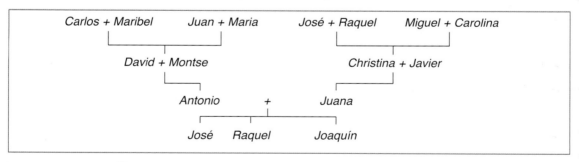

Exercise 2.6

¡Escucha!
¿Verdad o mentira?

	Verdad/Mentira
Hay 5 personas en su familia	
Su padre se llama Paco	
Su abuela se llama María	
Tiene 2 hermanos	
Carmen tiene 13 años	
El chico se llama Ricardo	

Los Verbos

Now the moment you've been waiting for: the Spanish verb! A verb, as you are probably well aware, is a "doing" word. Thus we can study, learn, play, eat and these are all verbs. If we put the word "to" in front of a verb in English we get its present infinitive, e.g. *to* study, *to* learn, etc. Spanish verbs have present infinitives, too, and the first type of Spanish verb that we are going to learn about consists of all those verbs which have an infinitive that ends in -*ar*, e.g. **hablar** = to speak, **visitar** = to visit, **estudiar** = to study, etc. We'll call them *AR* verbs. Note that to conjugate the verb, we remove the -*ar* and add a set of endings to the resulting stem.

Hablar = to speak				
	Singular		**Plural**	
1ˢᵗ person	*hablo*	I speak	*hablamos*	we speak
2ⁿᵈ person	*hablas*	you speak	*habláis*	you speak
3ʳᵈ person	*habla*	he/she/it speaks	*hablan*	they speak

Note that it is the verb **ending** which tells us who is doing the verb. There is no need for a subject pronoun, as there is in English, although of course these do exist (see page 30). And note that **all** regular *AR* verbs go like *hablar* and use these same endings (shown in red). A number of *AR* verbs are given in the *vocabulario* below.

So here's how they work:

Hablo español	=	I speak Spanish.
Compras un periódico	=	you buy a newspaper (**N.B.** just one of you).
Trabaja en un colegio	=	he (or she) works in a school.
Estudiamos inglés	=	we study English.
Visitáis España	=	you visit Spain (**N.B.** more than one of you).
Terminan los deberes	=	they finish their homework.

Exercise 2.7

¡Escribe en inglés!

1. *Hablamos inglés en el colegio.*
2. *Compran los periódicos.*
3. *Trabajo en la clase.*
4. *Estudiáis español en España.*
5. *Visito Gibraltar con mis amigos.*
6. *Miran al profesor y a la profesora.*
7. *Escuchas a tu hermano.*
8. *No termináis los deberes.*
9. *Los chicos no fuman en casa.*
10. *La chica visita a su abuelo.*

Vocabulario	
Visitar	= to visit
Estudiar	= to study
Trabajar	= to work
Comprar	= to buy
Terminar	= to finish
Mirar	= to watch
Fumar	= to smoke
Escuchar	= to listen

Note how, when the direct object of a verb is a **person** (rather than a thing), we add the word *a*.
E.g. *Miran **a** la profesora* = they look at the teacher.
Where *a* runs into *el* it becomes *al*.
E.g. *Miran **al** chico* = they look at the boy.

Exercise 2.8

¡Escribe en español!

Before we ask you to write some Spanish sentences of your own, just make sure that you are familiar with the way the endings are added to the stem of the verb you are using. Conjugate (write out) in full the following *AR* verbs, giving the meaning of each form.

1. *Visitar*
2. *Terminar*
3. *Escuchar*
4. *Trabajar*

The result should look very similar to the way *hablar* is laid out on the previous page.

Exercise 2.9

¡Escribe en español!

Note that if the subject of the sentence is a noun, the verb goes into the 3rd person.

E.g. The man (i.e. "he") works in an office = *el hombre trabaja en una oficina.*
       The pupils (i.e. "they") finish the homework = *los alumnos terminan los deberes.*

1. I visit Spain with my friend.
2. My brother works in the classroom.
3. The grandfather buys a newspaper.
4. My mother works in Madrid.
5. They study Spanish with the teacher.

Personal pronouns

As we have seen, the verb ending tells us who is doing a Spanish verb, and personal pronouns in Spanish are used only for emphasis. Notice that in most of these there is both a masculine and a feminine form.

	Singular		**Plural**	
1st person	*yo*	I	*nosotros / nosotras*	we
2nd person	*tú*	you	*vosotros / vosotras*	you
3rd person	*él / ella*	he/she	*ellos / ellas*	they

Note the accent on the pronoun *él* which distinguishes it from the definite article.

Exercise 2.10

¡Escucha, rellena los huecos y escribe en inglés!

1. — *escucho.*
2. — *estudias.*
3. — *trabaja pero — no trabaja.*
4. — *compra un periódico.*
5. — *visitamos al marido de Juana.*
6. — *visitamos a la mujer de Carlos.*
7. — *habláis con vuestra profesora.*
8. — *habláis con vuestro padre.*
9. — *miran al profesor.*
10. — *trabajan en un colegio.*

Exercise 2.11

¡Escribe!

In the following sentences choose which part of the verb is correct. Then translate.

1. *Yo compro / compramos un periódico.*
2. *La chica habla / hablas inglés.*
3. *Yo estudia / estudio en el colegio.*
4. *El profesor fuma / fumáis.*
5. *El abuelo visita / visitan Málaga.*
6. *Los hermanos escuchan / escuchas.*

Exercise 2.12

¡Escribe!

Here's another quick exercise to make sure you have fully understood before we move on to the next set of verbs. Add a verb that makes sense and write it in its correct form. Then translate.

1. *Nosotros — español.*
2. *Los alumnos — Málaga.*
3. *El hijo —*
4. *La mujer — en una oficina.*
5. *El chico y la chica — en la clase.*

Exercise 2.13

¡Escribe!

Now, enough of the gap-filling. Let's just translate the following. And watch those verb endings!

1. *Visitamos Barcelona.*
2. *Termina los deberes.*
3. *El chico compra un bolígrafo.*
4. *Estudiamos en el colegio.*
5. *Miramos la pizarra.*

6. I speak Spanish in class.
7. The pupils speak English at home.
8. The teacher does not smoke.
9. I buy a newspaper and some pens.
10. We work in a school.

Exercise 2.14

¡Habla!

Con tu amigo/amiga describe los dibujos:

En España

In England we refer to a ball-point pen as a biro. In Spain, they call it *un boli.*

Exercise 2.15

¡Habla y escribe!
Describe los dibujos.

Exercise 2.16

¡Escribe!
Rearrange the following verb forms in the correct order, starting with the infinitive:

1. *hablan habláis hablar habla hablo hablas hablamos*
2. *compra compro compráis compras compran compramos comprar*
3. *fumáis fumas fumamos fumar fuman fumo fuma*
4. *estudias estudio estudian estudiáis estudia estudiamos estudiar*
5. *mira mirar miro miráis miras miran miramos*

Usted y Ustedes

As we have seen, the polite form is used in Spanish with adults that one does not know well, rather like the *vous* form in French. *Usted* is often abbreviated to **Vd.**, itself an abbreviation of *Vuestra Merced* = your honour. *Ustedes* is often abbreviated to **Vds.**, an abbreviation of *Vuestras Mercedes* = your honours. This explains why it is the **3rd person** that is used in the polite forms because, for example, when one says to an adult "You are speaking", one is actually saying "Your honour is speaking"! Remember this, and you will never have trouble again with the polite forms in Spanish.

¿Trabaja usted en una oficina?

¿Visitan ustedes Sevilla?

ER Verbs

You now know how *AR* verbs work in Spanish and are ready to learn the next type, those having an infinitive which ends in *–er*.

Comer = to eat	Singular		Plural	
1ˢᵗ person	*como*	I eat	*comemos*	we eat
2ⁿᵈ person	*comes*	you eat	*coméis*	you eat
3ʳᵈ person	*come*	he/she/it eats	*comen*	they eat

As you can see, *ER* verbs follow a similar pattern to *AR* ones. The essential difference is the fact that the vowel in the ending is an *e* rather than an *a*; which is why they are called *ER* verbs!

Corro a la casa = I run to the house.
Leemos el periódico = we read the newspaper.
La mujer bebe cerveza = the woman drinks beer.
¿Conoce usted a mi mujer? = do you know my wife?

El hombre bebe cerveza.

> **Vocabulario**
> *Aprender* = to learn
> *Beber* = to drink
> *Comer* = to eat
> *Conocer* = to know (someone)
> *Correr* = to run
> *Leer* = to read

Exercise 2.17

¡Escribe!
Copy, selecting the correct part of the verb. Then translate into English.
1. *Mi marido bebe / beba / bebo cerveza.*
2. *Nosotras leemos / leéis / leen los libros.*
3. *El chico come / comen / coméis el chocolate.*
4. *Los españoles aprendéis / aprendan / aprenden inglés.*
5. *Mi abuela siempre corre / corren / corres a casa.*

Exercise 2.18

¡Escucha!
¿Qué hacen? = what are they doing?
Match up the answers A-F with the questions 1-4.
1. *Juan*
2. *Gloria*
3. *Cristóbal*
4. *Ricardo*

A. *estudia en el colegio.*
B. *come paella.*
C. *lee un libro.*
D. *bebe cerveza en la plaza.*
E. *aprende inglés.*
F. *lee un periódico en la plaza.*

Exercise 2.19

Now that you have met both *AR* verbs and *ER* ones, you need to take great care not to muddle them up. When you meet a new verb, learn its infinitive carefully as this will tell you how it goes. Now, give the present infinitive and meaning of:

1. *Bebemos*
2. *Coméis*
3. *Habláis*
4. *Miro*
5. *Corro*

6. *Leen*
7. *Hablan*
8. *Termino*
9. *Leo*
10. *Miramos*

Exercise 2.20

¡Habla!
Describe los dibujos.

Vocabulario 2.1

El abuelo	= the grandfather
El hermano	= the brother
El hijo	= the son
El hombre	= the man
El marido	= the husband
El nieto	= the grandson
El padrastro	= the step-father
El padre	= the father
El primo	= the cousin (masculine)
El tío	= the uncle
La abuela	= the grandmother
La familia	= the family
La hermana	= the sister
La hija	= the daughter
La madrastra	= the step-mother
La madre	= the mother
La mujer	= the wife, woman
La nieta	= the grand-daughter
La prima	= the cousin (feminine)
La tía	= the aunt
El colegio	= the school

Comprar	= to buy
Escuchar	= to listen
Estudiar	= to study
Fumar	= to smoke
Mirar	= to look at
Terminar	= to finish
Trabajar	= to work
Visitar	= to visit
Aprender	= to learn
Beber	= to drink
Comer	= to eat
Conocer	= to know (someone)
Correr	= to run
Leer	= to read
Ver	= to see
Mi	= my
Tu	= your
Su	= his, her
Siempre	= always

IR Verbs

I'm sure you've got the hang of the verbs you have met so far, so it's now time to look at the last set of regular verbs, known as *IR* verbs. As you would expect, *IR* verbs have a present infinitive ending in *–ir*. Note that the endings are the same as for *ER* verbs in all but the 1st and 2nd persons plural.

Vivir = to live

		Singular		Plural	
1st person	vivo	I live	vivimos	we live
2nd person	vives	you live	vivís	you live
3rd person	vive	he/she/it lives	viven	they live

Exercise 2.21

¡Escribe!

Complete, using the correct form of the verb in brackets.
Then translate:

Vocabulario
Escribir = to write
Recibir = to receive
Decidir = to decide
Cumplir = to reach the age of

1. *Yo (escribir) una carta*

2. *Tú (decidir) correr*

3. *Ella (cumplir) 11 años*

4. *Nosotros (escribir) una carta*

5. *Vosotras (cumplir) 15 años*

6. *Ellos (recibir) unos regalos*

Exercise 2.22

¡Escribe!
Now put the following into the plural.

Yo decido, for example, would become *nosotros decidimos*, because "we" is the plural of "I". "You (plural)" is the plural of "you (singular)" and "they" is the plural of "he" and "she".

1. *él decide*
2. *tú cumples*
3. *yo recibo*
4. *ella escribe*
5. *tú decides*
6. *usted escribe*

Exercise 2.23

¡Escribe!
Rearrange the following verb forms in the correct order, with the infinitive first:

1. *recibís, recibo, recibir, recibes, reciben, recibe, recibimos*
2. *viven, vives, vivimos, vivir, vivís, vivo, vive*
3. *cumple, cumplen, cumplo, cumplir, cumples, cumplís, cumplimos*
4. *decidís, decidir, decidimos, decido, decide, decides, deciden*
5. *escribes, escribís, escribo, escribimos, escribe, escriben, escribir*

Exercise 2.24

¡Lee y contesta las preguntas!

Mi padre se llama Juan y mi madre se llama Carolina. Vivimos en Toledo que está a 50 kilómetros de Madrid. Tengo un hermano que se llama Pedro y una hermana que se llama Dolores.

1. *El padre .... Juan.*
2. *La ....es Carolina.*
3. *Madrid está a ....
   kilómetros de Toledo.*
4. *Pedro es ....*
5. *La hermana .... Dolores.*

Toledo

Irregular verbs: tener

We have now learnt that the endings of verbs follow a regular pattern which can be learnt quite easily. Once you have learnt this pattern, whether it is an *AR, ER* or *IR* verb, you can use if for countless numbers of other verbs. However, some verbs are irregular. Irregular verbs are a law unto themselves and have some weird forms which you simply have to learn by heart as quickly as possible. One such verb is *tener* = to have.

Tener

We have already met the first three forms, *tengo, tienes* and *tiene*. Here it is now in all its glory:

Tener = to have				
	Singular		**Plural**	
1st person	*tengo*	I have	*tenemos*	we have
2nd person	*tienes*	you have	*tenéis*	you have
3rd person	*tiene*	he/she/it has	*tienen*	they have

As we have already seen, one of the ways in which we use *tener* is when giving our ages. Thus in Spanish, as in French, one *has* an age rather than *being* an age.

E.g.   *Gloria tiene 14 años.*
E.g.   *Roberto y Elena tienen 14 años.*

Exercise 2.25

¡Escucha y rellena los huecos!

1.   *Juan tiene — años. Juan es el — de Carolina.*
2.   *Gloria tiene — años. Gloria es la — de Carolina.*
3.   *— — 31años. — es el — de Carolina.*
4.   *José y — tienen — años. Son los — de Carolina.*
5.   *Los hermanastros — y — tienen — y — años. Viven con el — en —.*

Exercise 2.26

¡Escribe en inglés!

1.   *Juan tiene un bolígrafo.*
2.   *Tenemos un profesor magnífico.*
3.   *María y Ricardo tienen una casa en Badajoz.*
4.   *Tenéis una casa en Cáceres.*
5.   *¿Cuándo tienes la clase de español?*

Ser

The verb *ser* = 'to be' is another irregular verb, but if you know any French (or Latin) you should have no difficulty sorting out its various forms:

Ser = to be				
	Singular		**Plural**	
1st person	*soy*	I am	*somos*	we are
2nd person	*eres*	you are	*sois*	you are
3rd person	*es*	he/she/it is	*son*	they are

Exercise 2.27

¡Escribe en inglés!
Study the verb ser carefully. Then translate into English:

1. *Soy un alumno.*
2. *Juan es profesor.*
3. *Somos estudiantes.*

4. *Eres mi amigo.*
5. *Son mis abuelos.*
6. *Ella es mi madre.*

Exercise 2.28

¡Escribe en español!

1. Juan is a student.
2. María and Francisco are my grandparents.
3. They are my friends.
4. She is a pupil.
5. You are my students.
6. I am your teacher.

"Ser, o no ser, ésa es la cuestión."

Los adjetivos

To describe someone, or something, we need to use adjectives. It may have come as a shock to learn that nouns are either masculine, feminine, singular, or plural. The next shock is to discover that adjectives in Spanish **have to agree with the noun that they are describing!** This means that if the noun is masculine, the adjective must be masculine; if the noun is feminine, the adjective must be feminine; if the noun is singular, the adjective must be singular; and if the noun is plural, the adjective must be plural.

The changes that occur in the adjectives can be predicted depending on the masculine singular form of the adjective.

1. Adjectives which end in *o*; e.g. *bonito* = beautiful, pretty

	Singular	**Plural**
Masculine	*bonito*	*bonitos*
Feminine	*bonita*	*bonitas*
E.g.	*Un pueblo bonito*	*Unos pueblos bonitos*
E.g.	*Una ciudad bonita*	*Unas ciudades bonitas*

2. Adjectives which end in *a*; e.g. *optimista* = optimistic, hopeful

	Singular	**Plural**
Masculine	*optimista*	*optimistas*
Feminine	*optimista*	*optimistas*
E.g.	*Un chico optimista*	*Unos chicos optimistas*
E.g.	*Una chica optimista*	*Unas chicas optimistas*

These are very simple, as there is no difference between the masculine and feminine forms.

3. Adjectives which end in *e* or a consonant; e.g. *grande* = big; *azul* = blue

	Singular	**Plural**
Masculine	*grande; azul*	*grandes; azules*
Feminine	*grande; azul*	*grandes; azules*
E.g.	*Un edificio grande*	*Unos edificios grandes*
E.g.	*Una casa grande*	*Unas casas grandes*

Note again that, with these adjectives, there is no difference between the masculine and the feminine forms.

Finally, now that you have seen all the various adjectives at work, note how adjectives in Spanish normally come AFTER the noun they describe.

¿Cómo eres?

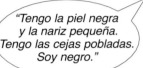

"Tengo el pelo negro y corto y los ojos castaños. Soy moreno."

"Tengo la cara redonda y las orejas pequeñas. Soy rubia."

"Tengo el pelo largo y rizado, y los ojos azules. Soy pelirroja."

"Tengo la piel negra y la nariz pequeña. Tengo las cejas pobladas. Soy negro."

Vocabulario

El ojo	= the eye	Grande	= big
El pelo	= the hair	Guapo	= handsome / pretty
La cara	= the face	Largo	= long
La ceja	= the eye-brow	Marrón	= brown
La nariz	= the nose	Moreno	= dark
La oreja	= the ear	Negro	= black
La piel	= the skin	Pelirrojo	= redhead
Alto	= tall	Pequeño	= small
Antipático	= unpleasant/horrible	Perezoso	= lazy
Azul	= blue	Pesado	= annoying
Bajo	= short	Poblado	= bushy
Blanco	= white	Redondo	= round
Cariñoso	= loving, affectionate	Rizado	= curly
Castaño	= brown, chestnut	Rubio	= blonde
Corto	= short	Simpático	= kind, nice
Delgado	= thin	Trabajador	= hardworking
Gordo	= fat	Vago	= lazy

Exercise 2.29

¡Escucha y rellena los huecos!

1. El chico se llama —.
2. Vive en —.
3. Tiene — años.
4. Hay — personas en su familia.
5. Su padre se llama —.
6. Su madre se llama —.
7. Ana María es su —.
8. Javier tiene — años.
9. Su madre tiene — años.
10. Su madre tiene los — verdes.
11. Su hermana tiene — años.
12. Su hermana tiene el pelo — .

Exercise 2.30

¡Escribe!

Using the information you have learnt about adjective agreement, select the correct form of the adjective and then translate:

1. *Un profesor baja / bajos / bajo*
2. *Una profesora antipática / antipático / antipáticas*
3. *Unos hermanos pesado / pesadas / pesados*
4. *Unas hermanas pesado / pesadas / pesados*
5. *La abuela delgados / delgada / delgadas*
6. *Un chico cariñosa / cariñoso / cariñosas*
7. *Una chica guapo / guapas / guapa*
8. *Un instituto grande / grandes / grando*
9. *Los estudiantes trabajadores / trabajadoras / trabajadoros*
10. *Unos abuelos simpáticos / simpáticas / simpátices*

Exercise 2.31

¡Habla!
¿Cómo eres?

Try to describe yourself to your partner, using the words and phrases you have learned so far.

Exercise 2.32

¡Lee y contesta en inglés!

Mis amigos son españoles y viven en Guadalupe. Juan está muy gordo pero Gloria está delgada. Mi profesor de español es muy cariñoso mientras que mi profesor de inglés es muy pesado.

1. The nationality of my friends is ....
2. The fat person is called ....
3. The thin person is called ....
4. My Spanish teacher is ....
5. My English teacher, however, is ....

¡Hola! Me llamo Gloria.

¿Tienes animales en casa?

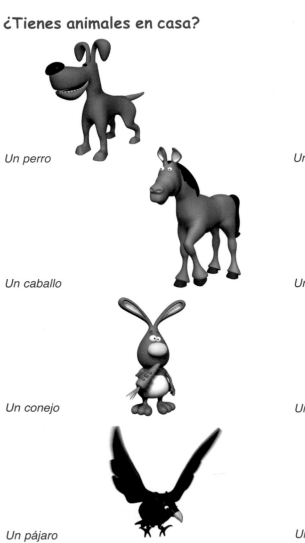

Un perro

Un gato

Un caballo

Un hámster

Un conejo

Un pez

Un pájaro

Un ratón

Una tortuga

Un burro

Una araña

Una vaca

Exercise 2.33

¡Habla!
¿Qué es?
How quickly can you identify (in Spanish) the pets that you have learnt? Use photos or pictures of different pets to test your recognition skills.

Exercise 2.34

Lee y escucha el diálogo y contesta las preguntas:

Roberto: *¿Tienes animales en casa?*
Rafael: *Sí, tengo un gato, dos perros y una tortuga.*

Roberto: *¿Cómo se llama tu tortuga?*
Rafael: *Se llama Matilde y es muy cariñosa.*

Roberto: *¿Y tus perros – cómo son?*
Rafael: *Uno es grande y blanco; se llama Gigante. El otro es pequeño, muy delgado y marrón; se llama Lucho. Y tú – ¿no tienes animales?*

Roberto: *¡Sí claro! Tengo una mantis religiosa!*
Rafael: *¡Qué miedo!*

1. *¿Cuántos animales tiene Rafael?*
2. *¿Quién tiene una tortuga?*
3. *¿Cómo es la tortuga?*
4. *¿De qué color son los perros de Rafael?*
5. *¿Cómo se llaman los perros?*
6. *¿Qué animal tiene Roberto?*

Exercise 2.35

¡Habla!
Con tu amigo / amiga, describe tus animales.

Vocabulario

El animal	= animal, pet	*La araña*	= spider
El burro	= donkey	*La mantis religiosa*	= praying mantis
El caballo	= horse	*La mascota*	= pet
El conejo	= rabbit	*La tortuga*	= tortoise
El gato	= cat	*La vaca*	= cow
El hámster	= hamster	*El otro*	= the other
El léon	= lion	*¡Sí claro!*	= yes of course!
El pájaro	= bird	*¡Qué miedo!*	= how scary!
El perro	= dog	*¿Quién?*	= who?
El pez	= fish		
El ratón	= mouse		

Exercise 2.36

¡Escucha y completa las frases!

1. *En casa David tiene dos — y — perro.*
2. *El perro se llama —.*
3. *El perro tiene — años.*
4. *Dolores vive en —.*
5. *Dolores tiene un —.*
6. *Es — y tiene — años.*
7. *Héctor es el — de —.*
8. *Héctor es — y blanco.*
9. *En la casa de María hay —.*
10. *Rapidez es una —.*

Exercise 2.37

¡Escribe en español!

1. Here is my father. Here is his dog.
2. My cat is called Senta.
3. Here are my cousins. Their dogs are called Pastor and Alemán.
4. Hello David. Where is your tortoise?
5. Here are Dolores and Antonio. How many pets do they have?

Exercise 2.38

¡Escribe!

Rellena los huecos y escribe en inglés, como en el ejemplo:

1. *"Yo __soy__ profesor"* =
I am a teacher.

2. *"¡Usted ____ un profesor magnífico!"*

3. *"Mi amigo _____ el hijo del profesor."*

4. *"Nosotros _____ los campeones."*

5. *"Vosotros _____ los vencidos."*

> **Note**
> When saying what one is in the 1st person, e.g. I am a teacher, the article is omitted. E.g. *Yo soy profesor.*

Exercise 2.39

¡Escribe en español!

1. She has a black horse.
2. We are friends of John and Christine.
3. I am a teacher.*
4. This is my brother's dog.
5. They are the parents of José.

*Remember not to use the article!

Exercise 2.41

¡Escribe en inglés!

1. *Mi padre se llama Juan. Es bastante alto y muy trabajador.*
2. *Mi amigo es muy perezoso pero muy simpático.*
3. *El profesor de español es bastante alto, muy simpático y muy guapo.*
4. *El profesor de francés es bajo, está muy gordo y de vez en cuando es antipático.*

Exercise 2.40

¡Escribe en español!

1. My sister is ten years old.
2. I am from Barcelona.
3. We have two rabbits and one hamster.
4. My uncle is from Madrid.
5. We have a wonderful grandmother.

Vocabulario
De vez en cuando = from time to time
Muy = very
Bastante = quite

Exercise 2.42

¡Escribe!

Take the sentences in the previous exercise and change them so that all the nouns are feminine. A father thus becomes a mother; a brother becomes a sister, etc. Remember that the adjectives will also change.

Exercise 2.43

¡Escribe en inglés!

1. *Tú tienes un marido español.*
2. *Soy grande y trabajador.*
3. *Eres bajo y gordo.*
4. *Mi amigo es francés y vago.*
5. *Mi hermano es simpático y cariñoso.*

Exercise 2.44

¡Escribe en inglés!

Take the sentences in the previous exercise and change them so that all the nouns (and pronouns) are plural. 'A book' will become 'some books', 'I' will become 'we', 'he' will become 'they', etc.
Remember again that the adjectives will change, as will the definite or indefinite articles and the verbs.

Los colores

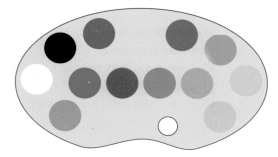

Vocabulario	
Blanco	= white
Dorado	= golden
Negro	= black
Rojo	= red
Amarillo	= yellow
Morado	= purple
Plateado	= silver
Naranja	= orange
Rosa	= pink
Azul	= blue
Verde	= green
Marrón	= brown
Gris	= grey

Exercise 2.45

¡Escucha!
Subraya los colores correctos en la ficha, como en el ejemplo.
Ejemplo: La hierba es verde.

La hierba	verde
El cielo	–
El sol	–
El hámster	–
El caballo	–
La nieve	–

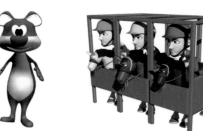

La corrida de toros

Bullfighting has been taking place in Spain, in its present format, since the 12th Century. There are many people in Spain who are opposed to the *espectáculo*, as they believe that it's cruel and barbaric, although most major cities and towns do have a bullring. Read on, and see what you think…

There is always a procession before the fight begins when the *matadores* (the men who kill the bulls) lead out their teams (*las cuadrillas*, consisting of *picadores, banderilleros* and *peones*) and salute the president (*el presidente*).

On the sound of a trumpet (*el clarín*), the bull will enter the ring where the *matador* and *peones* "test" it with the cape (*el capote*). This is to see if the bull charges in a straight line, attacks with the left or right horn, etc. After about two minutes, two *picadores* enter the ring on horseback and incite the bull to charge. As the bull charges, the *picadores* try to stick a lance in the bull's neck. Two *banderilleros* then stick six long darts (*banderillas*) into the same area of the bull's neck as the bull charges towards them.

The *matador* then takes centre stage, dedicates the bull to a friend, his wife or girlfriend, his manager or the crowd, and incites the bull to charge with the famous red cape *la muleta*. He now performs, to the best of his ability, various passes, always, however, trying to stand erect, his feet together and drawing the bull closer and closer to his body. After about 15 minutes he kills the bull with a sword (*una espada*) and this act is the *estocada*.

Depending on how brave the *matador* has been, the complexity of his moves with the cape, and his ability to kill cleanly, he may be awarded the ear (*la oreja*) of the dead bull. If he has been exceptionally good, he will be awarded the two ears and in exceptional circumstances, the tail (*el rabo*). Depending on how many times the *matador* has fought and the number of ears and tails he has been awarded, his position on the *escalfón* or "league table" is decided . Top *matadores* can earn around €150,000 for a big fight in the bullring.

Exercise 2.46

¡Escribe!
Completa cada frase con una palabra:

1. *El toro es ....*
2. *La chaqueta de El Juli es ....*
3. *La corbata es ....*
4. *La muleta es .... y ....*

Exercise 2.47

¡Habla! ¿Cuál es tu color preferido?
Ejemplo: Mi color preferido es el naranja.

Vocabulario

El toro	= bull
La chaqueta	= jacket
La corbata	= neck-tie
La muleta	= cape

Exercise 2.48

¡Lee y contesta en inglés!

Aquí tenemos a El Juli. El Juli es uno de los matadores más famosos en España. Su apodo es El Juli. Se llama Julián López Escobar. Su madre es de Toledo y su padre es de Jaén. Tiene dos hermanos. El mayor se llama Manolo y el otro se llama Ignacio. Hoy torea en la plaza de toros de México. Ésta es la plaza mas grande del mundo. Lleva una chaqueta de oro y calcetines blancos. El Juli es muy famoso en México. Los aficionados gritan "¡Venga, vamos El Juli!" Después de la corrida va a un hotel y cena con sus amigos.

1. Who is Julián López Escobar?
2. What is his nickname?
3. Who are Manoli and Ignacio?
4. Why is Mexico mentioned?
5. What is its claim to fame?
6. What is El Juli wearing?
7. Who shouts "Come on, El Juli!"?
8. What does El Juli do after the bullfight?

Exercise 2.49

¡Escribe una frase de 5-8 palabras sobre cada uno de estos dibujos, como en el ejemplo:

Ejemplo: Mi hermano tiene un caballo grande.

Mi madre tiene…

Mi abuela tiene…

Mi hermana tiene…

Mi tía tiene…

Mi amigo tiene…

¿Por qué aprender el español?

Did you know that:

- Spanish is the second most widely-spoken language in the world, used by more than 450 million people?
- Around 11% of the population of the USA use Spanish as their first language?
- Spanish is the language spoken in the world's largest city, Mexico City?
- Many famous US cities have Spanish names: Los Angeles, San Francisco, Colorado etc.?
- America used to be known simply as Florida? What does *florida* mean in Spanish?

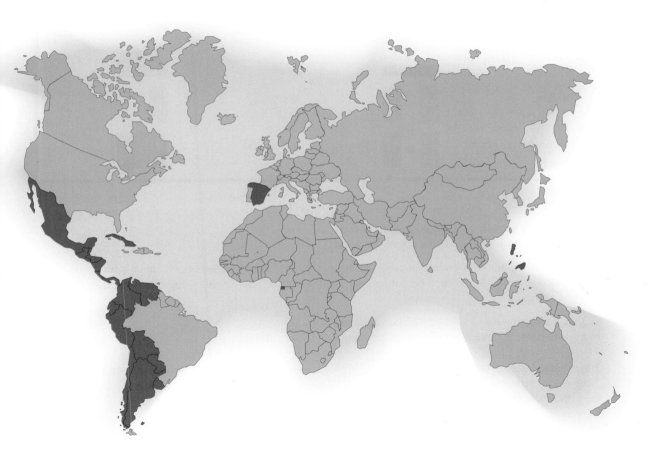

Spanish-speaking countries are shown in red.

Las nacionalidades

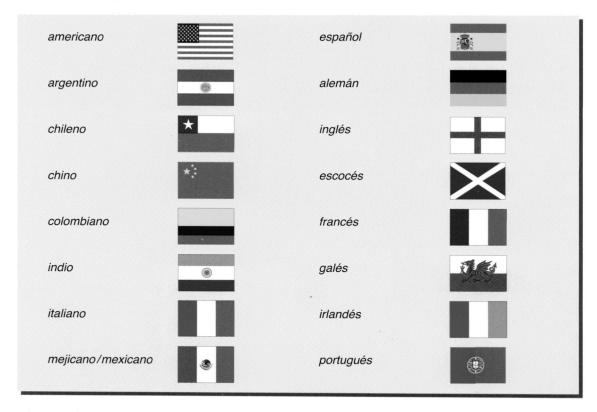

americano	español
argentino	alemán
chileno	inglés
chino	escocés
colombiano	francés
indio	galés
italiano	irlandés
mejicano/mexicano	portugués

Nationalities are, of course, adjectives, and behave as such.

E.g. *Un chico italiano*   *Unos chicos italianos*
E.g. *Una chica italiana*   *Unas chicas italianas*

But note that nationalities ending in a consonant, e.g. *inglés, español, alemán*, etc. have a feminine form which ends in *–a* (i.e. they do not behave like the normal adjectives ending in a consonant which you have met).

E.g. *Un chico inglés*   *Unos chicos ingleses*
E.g. *Una chica inglesa*   *Unas chicas inglesas*

Note that the accent on words such as *inglés, francés, escocés* etc only occurs in the masculine singular. Note also (in case you have forgotten) that nationalities in Spanish do not begin with a capital letter as they do in English.

Exercise 2.50

¡Escribe en inglés!

1. *Juan es español.*
2. *Los profesores son portugueses.*
3. *Mi amigo irlandés es vago.*
4. *Mi amigo español es cariñoso.*
5. *Mis profesores ingleses son trabajadores.*
6. *David es galés.*
7. *Mi profesora de inglés está gorda.*
8. *Mi profesor de español es guapo.*
9. *Mi hermano es pesado.*
10. *Muchos españoles son cariñosos.*

Exercise 2.51

¡Escribe en español!
1. Are you Spanish?
2. This is José. He is Portugese.
3. My parents are French.
4. My teacher is American.
5. Five pupils in my class are English, three are Irish and two are Welsh.
6. Seven pupils are Scottish, nine are Indian and two are Chinese.
7. My mother is French and my father is Italian.
8. Here are my friends, Juan and Cristina. They are Spanish.*

Note
*When making an adjective agree with nouns of different genders, the masculine form is used.

Exercise 2.52

¡Lee y escucha!

Hola. Me llamo Ignacio y soy de Madrid. Soy alto y deportista pero según mis amigos soy vago de vez en cuando.

Hola. Soy Teresa y vivo en Sevilla. Hay cinco personas en mi familia. Mi padre, mi madre, mi hermano, mi hermana y yo. Mi hermano mayor se llama Jorge y es muy gordo. Mi hermana menor se llama Nuria y ¡es muy pesada!

Yo soy Eduardo y tengo veinticuatro años. Vivo en una casa muy grande en el centro de Madrid. Soy rubio con los ojos castaños. Mi padre es español pero mi madre es argentina. Mi madre es guapa y simpática. Mi novia se llama María. Es morena.

¡Buenos días! Me llamo Elizabeth y soy inglesa pero vivo en España. Somos tres en la familia – mis padres y yo. Vivimos en un apartamento grande en Toledo. Mis padres son muy simpáticos. Mi madre es alta y delgada. Mi padre es bajo.

What information do we learn about the following?

1. *Ignacio*
2. *Teresa*
3. *Eduardo*
4. *Elizabeth*

Exercise 2.53

¡Habla!
Answer the following questions. Include nationality in your answers.
Note that *tu* (without an accent) means "your" whereas *tú* with an accent means you.

1. *¿Cómo es tu padre?*
2. *¿Cómo es tu madre?*
3. *¿Cómo eres?*
4. *¿Cómo es tu profesor/a de español?*
5. *¿Cómo es tu director/a?*
6. *¿Cómo es tu mejor amigo/a?*

Vocabulario	
El director	= headmaster
La directora	= headmistress
Mejor	= best
Según	= according to

Exercise 2.54

¡Escucha!

¿Qué idioma hablas?

N.B. *El castellano* = Castilian (the form of Spanish used in most parts of Spain and in South America).
El catalán = Catalan (the language spoken in *Cataluña*)

1. *Carlos*
2. *Juanita*
3. *Patricia*

4. *David*
5. *Monique*
6. *Ralph*

Exercise 2.55

¡Lee!

¿Quién es? ¡Adivina estos personajes famosos españoles!

1. *Es un hombre famoso en la literatura española. Es muy alto y muy delgado. Tiene un caballo que se llama Rocinante. Tiene también un amigo muy gordo que se llama Sancho. ¿Quién es?*

2. *Es un famoso pintor español. Se llama Pablo y vive en Málaga en 1881. Es un hombre bajo y está bastante gordo. Vive también en París. Pinta un cuadro famoso que se llama Guernica. ¿Quién es?*

3. *Su nombre es Cristóbal. Es un famoso navegante español. Vive en España y Portugal. En 1492 descubre Cuba y La Española. ¿Quién es?*

Vocabulario 2.2

Escribir	= to write	*El animal*	= animal, pet
Recibir	= to receive	*El caballo*	= horse
Decidir	= to decide	*El conejo*	= rabbit
Cumplir	= to reach the age of	*El gato*	= cat
Ser	= to be	*El hámster*	= hamster
Tener	= to have	*El pájaro*	= bird
		El perro	= dog
El ojo	= eye	*El pez*	= fish
El pelo	= hair	*El ratón*	= mouse
La cara	= face	*La araña*	= spider
La nariz	= nose	*La tortuga*	= tortoise
La oreja	= ear		
La piel	= skin	*Amarillo*	= yellow
		Blanco	= white
Alto	= tall	*Negro*	= black
Antipático	= horrible	*Rojo*	= red
Bajo	= short	*Naranja*	= orange
Cariñoso	= loving	*Rosa*	= pink
Delgado	= thin	*Azul*	= blue
Gordo	= fat	*Verde*	= green
Grande	= big	*Marrón*	= brown
Guapo	= handsome / pretty	*Gris*	= grey
Otro	= other		
Pesado	= annoying	*¿Quién?*	= who?
Pequeño	= small	*Ahora*	= now
Simpático	= kind, nice	*Bastante*	= quite
Trabajador	= hardworking	*Muy*	= very
Vago	= lazy	*También*	= also

Los números 30–100

Now for some more numbers:

30	*Treinta*	40	*Cuarenta*
31	*Treinta y uno*	41	*Cuarenta y uno*
32	*Treinta y dos*	42	*Cuarenta y dos*
33	*Treinta y tres*		
34	*Treinta y cuatro*	50	*Cincuenta*
35	*Treinta y cinco*	60	*Sesenta*
36	*Treinta y seis*	70	*Setenta*
37	*Treinta y siete*	80	*Ochenta*
38	*Treinta y ocho*	90	*Noventa*
39	*Treinta y nueve*	100	*Cien*

Exercise 2.56

¡Escribe en español!
1. Eighty seven
2. Seventy six
3. Sixty five
4. Ninety two
5. Forty four

Exercise 2.57

¡Escribe en inglés!
1. *Treinta y dos*
2. *Cuarenta y uno*
3. *Noventa y cuatro*
4. *Setenta y cinco*
5. *Cincuenta y seis*

Exercise 2.58

¡Habla!
Explain in Spanish how you could arrive at the number in **green**, using the 4 numbers underneath.
You can add (*más*), subtract, (*menos*), multiply (*multiplicado por*) and divide (*dividido por*).

Por ejemplo:

21

(3 ? 6) ? 9 ? 6

Possible answer: (3x6) + 9 - 6 = 21

46	**40**	**43**	**67**	**76**
2 ? 4 ? 21 ? 33	9 ? 7 ? 4 ? 2	16 ? 23 ? 4 ? 5	2 ? 14 ? 19 ? 74	6 ? 7 ? 8 ? 62

After doing the above I hope that you have learnt *sum*thing about Spanish numbers…

¿Cuál es tu número de teléfono?

Giving your telephone number correctly to someone you have just met on the beach can be really quite important, so we had better practise this now.

Exercise 2.59

¡Escucha y escribe los números de teléfono!

1. *Carolina*
2. *Miguel*
3. *Francisco*
4. *Antonio*

Ficha personal

Nombre:	*Cristóbal*
Apellidos*:	*Fernández García*
Dirección:	*Vía Roma 5-5º* *43840 SALOU* *España*
Edad:	*14*
Fecha de nacimiento:	*23 de abril de 1987*
Nacionalidad:	*española*

* **N.B.** All Spanish people have two surnames; the first is their father's and the second their mother's.

Exercise 2.60

¡Lee!
1. *¿Cómo se apellida Cristóbal (el nombre completo)?*
2. *¿Dónde vive?*
3. *¿Cuántos años tiene?*
4. *¿Cuándo es su cumpleaños?*
5. *¿De dónde es?*

> **Vocabulario**
> *Nació* = born
> *Exped.* (*expedido*) = issued
> *Val.* (*válido*) = valid
> *Domicilio* = residence
> *Localidad* = locality
> *Provincia* = province

Exercise 2.61

Lee y contesta las preguntas:

1. *¿Cómo se apellida esta chica?*
2. *¿Dónde nació?*
3. *¿Cuándo es su cumpleaños?*
4. *¿Cuántos años tiene?*

5. *¿Cómo se llama su padre?*
6. *¿Cómo se llama su madre?*
7. *¿Dónde vive?*

Exercise 2.62

¡Escucha y rellena las fichas!

1. *Chica A*
2. *Chico A*
3. *Chico B*
4. *Chica B*

> **Vocabulario**
> *La calle* = the street
> *El piso* = the floor

Exercise 2.63

Repaso de vocabulario

1. *Escribe las palabras siguientes bajo el título correspondiente:*

•rotulador •español •rojo •alemán •enero ,naranja •pizarra •silla
•noviembre ,domingo •lunes primavera ,inglés •diciembre , regla
•argentino verano •gris ,julio jueves •bolígrafo invierno

meses	días	estaciones	colores	equipo	nacionalidades

2. *¡Habla!*

Compara tus respuestas.

E.g. *¿Qué tienes en "equipo"?*

En equipo yo tengo bolígrafo y pizarra.

Possession

You will (I'm sure) have noticed that in Spanish there is no "apostrophe s", as there is in English. To indicate possession, then, we always have to use the word "of", i.e. **de**:

E.g. John's book = the book of John
El libro de Juan

E.g. Mary's ruler = the ruler of Mary
La regla de María

N.B. where the word **de** runs into the word **el**, the result is **del**:

E.g. The teacher's book = *el libro **del** profesor.*

Exercise 2.64

Traduce al español:

1. Francisco's mother.
2. Elena's teachers.
3. My aunt's daughter.
4. Your friend's family (familiar form).
5. His sister's schoolbag.
6. The boy's biro.
7. The girl's ruler.
8. My parents' books.
9. The pupils' scissors.
10. Her friend's homework.

Exercise 2.65

¿Cómo se dice en español?

1. My father's name is Robert.
2. My grandfather is called Angel.
3. Maribel is Gloria's grand-daughter
4. Rafael is my step-brother.
5. Her uncle David is her mother's brother.
6. Jorge is Miguel's son.

La Navidad

In Spain, Christmas is celebrated in quite a different way from England. The festivities begin on Christmas Eve (*LA NOCHEBUENA*) with a traditional supper, which is often *BESUGO AL HORNO* (baked sea-bream), but this can vary from region to region. After the meal it is customary for most Spaniards to attend midnight Mass – *LA MISA DEL GALLO*.

Spanish people decorate their homes with a nativity scene – *UN BELÉN* – ranging from the home-made variety to more sophisticated models – including little figures of Joseph, Mary, the baby Jesus, the shepherds, the three kings and various animals. It is now becoming quite popular for Spanish homes to have a Christmas tree as well, although this is not a traditional Spanish custom.

On the 25th December – *EL DÍA DE NAVIDAD* – families spend the day quietly together at home. After the meal, which can consist of roast turkey – *PAVO ASADO* – or shellfish – *MARISCOS* – they eat a variety of different nougat sweets – *TURRÓN* – and little marzipan figures – *FIGURITAS DE MAZAPÁN*.

New Year's Eve – *LA NOCHEVIEJA* – is celebrated in style, and it is the season of the year when the price of grapes rises astronomically, given the fact that each person in the family has to have 12 grapes ready to eat at each chime of the clock at midnight! In Madrid, particularly, crowds gather in the streets, especially in the *PUERTA DEL SOL*, a focal point in the centre of town where there is a large clock that chimes on the hour. Everybody has his or her supply of grapes, which are usually washed down with champagne – *CAVA*. People dance and sing and the fun goes on until the early hours of the morning.

Spanish children have to wait a long time for their presents, which are delivered by the three kings – *LOS TRES REYES MAGOS* – on the 6th January, commonly known as *EL DÍA DE REYES*. Instead of leaving a stocking out for their presents, they put out their shoes. If a child is naughty, he or she is given a piece of coal, but this is not a real problem, as it is of the edible variety that you can buy at the local pastry shop!

In many Spanish towns there are Christmas processions or *CABALGATAS* with the three kings – *MELCHOR, GASPAR* and *BALTASAR* – who are dressed up in all their finery. On the day of the Kings it is a custom to eat *EL ROSCÓN DE REYES*, which is a kind of large sweet cake with angelica on it containing a little charm. The cake is cut into individual pieces and the person who receives the charm is the king or queen for the day.

> **Vocabulario**
> *Feliz Navidad* or *Felices Fiestas* =
>   Happy Christmas
> *Feliz Año Nuevo* = Happy New year.

Deberes

Find out as much as you can about how Christmas is celebrated in a Spanish-speaking country of your choice. Present your findings to the rest of your class, for example as a Powerpoint presentation.

Expectations

At the end of this unit

You should understand and respond to descriptions of family members, including basic appearance and nationality; talk and write about families, friends and pets; count up to 100; spell the words from this unit; be more confident in the use of dictionaries to help you understand language and find new words; distinguish between *¿Quién? ¿Qué? ¿Cómo?* and *¿Cuántos/as?*; understand when and how to use different verb endings; distinguish between definite and indefinite articles.

You might also be able to: use a range of questions and answers in a conversation; read short passages and infer meanings from contexts; write a passage of Spanish, using a range of adjectives.

About the unit

In this unit you will learn to talk about which school subjects you like, dislike and prefer, giving simple reasons. You will learn to comment orally and in writing about your school timetable and the times of different activities, including mealtimes. You will extend your learning about how to use a dictionary or glossary, and enhance memory work.

New contexts:

- school subjects and timetables
- telling the time
- mealtimes and simple items of food and drink

New language content:

- expressing likes, dislikes and preferences using *(no) gustar (mucho, nada)*
- radical- (stem) changing verbs *e → ie*, eg *preferir (ie)* and *pensar (ie)*
- adverbs of frequency *(normalmente, siempre, algunas* veces)
- asking the question *¿A qué hora?*
- the irregular verb *hacer*

Las asignaturas

We are now going to look at the subjects we study at school. As ever, take care to learn the spelling of these words carefully, accents and all.

El alemán

El español

El francés

El inglés

El latín

El dibujo

Los deportes

La química

La biología

La física

La historia

La informática

La música

La religión

La tecnología

La educación física

La geografía

Las matemáticas

N.B. *Los idiomas* = languages; *Las ciencias* = sciences.

Exercise 3.1

¡Escucha!
Escribe las asignaturas preferidas de
1. *Mónica*
2. *Fernando*

3. *Teresa*
4. *Ignacio*

Exercise 3.2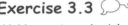

¡Lee y escribe en inglés!
1. *Yo estudio muchas asignaturas. El inglés es útil, la física es aburrida pero soy fuerte en historia porque el profesor explica muy bien.*
2. *Mi asignatura preferida es la geografía porque es muy fácil.*
3. *¡Se me da fatal el francés!*
4. *Yo creo que las matemáticas son muy interesantes*, pero creo que el inglés es muy aburrido.*
5. *Se me da bien la historia. Creo que es interesante y me llevo bien con el profesor.*

***N.B.** Because mathematics is plural in Spanish, both the verb and the adjective are plural.

Vocabulario

Aburrido = boring	*Explicar* = to explain
Divertido = funny/amusing	*Me llevo bien con* = I get on well with
Fácil = easy	*Se me da* bien* = I'm good at
Fatal = dreadful	*Se me da* fatal* = I'm bad at
Interesante = interesting	*Ser fuerte en* = to be good at
Preferido = favourite	*Ser bueno en* = to be good at
Útil = useful	
Creer que = to believe/think that	* In the plural this becomes *se me dan*.
	E.g. *Se me dan bien las matemáticas.*

Exercise 3.3

¡Habla con tu amigo/a!
Completa las frases, como en el ejemplo:
Ejemplo: "Yo estudio 9 asignaturas. Mi asignatura preferida son las matemáticas porque son muy útiles. Se me da fatal el latín porque es aburrido."

1. *Yo estudio _____ asignaturas.*
2. *Mi asignatura preferida es _____ porque _____*
3. *Se me _____ fatal _____ porque _____*

Exercise 3.4

¡Lee y escribe en inglés!
1. *José estudia la geografía y las ciencias pero su asignatura preferida es el francés.*
2. *Cristina estudia las matemáticas y la física pero su asignatura preferida es la informática.*
3. *Juan y Pepe estudian muchas asignaturas. La asignatura preferida de Juan es el inglés y la asignatura preferida de Pepe es el francés.*
4. *Miguel cree que las matemáticas son muy divertidas porque son muy fáciles.*
5. *¡Hola! Me llamo María. Yo estudio muchas asignaturas. Se me dan fatal el alemán y el latín pero creo que las matemáticas son muy interesantes y muy útiles.*

Gustar

Now for something a bit strange. Believe it or not, we cannot say *we like* something in Spanish. We have to say that something *is pleasing to us* and the verb that we use is *gustar*.

So, to say "I like Spanish", we say: *me gusta el español* (literally = to me is pleasing Spanish). To say "you like Spanish", we say *te gusta el español*, and to say "he" or "she likes Spanish", we say *le gusta el español*. In doing this we are using indirect pronouns, which look suspiciously like the reflexive pronouns we mentioned earlier. Here they are in full:

	Singular	Plural
1st person	*me*	*nos*
2nd person	*te*	*os*
3rd person	*le*	*les*

Ejemplos:
Me gusta la historia
Te gusta el dibujo
Le gusta el inglés
Nos gusta la geografía
Os gustan las matemáticas
Les gusta el español

¡Me gusta el chocolate!

Note (again) that subjects such as *las matemáticas* which are plural in Spanish, *are* pleasing (i.e. *gustan* is plural). Obviously to say that we don't like something we simply use *no* = not.
E.g. *No me gusta la historia* = I don't like history.
E.g. *No te gustan las matemáticas* = You don't like maths.

Extra things to note about gustar (not for the faint-hearted!)

1. In the 3rd person, if we are using a noun (rather than a pronoun), we must insert "*a*" (= to) before the noun and use the indirect pronoun *le* (singular) or *les* (plural).

*A Juan **le** gusta la música*　　　　　　(literally: **to** Juan, music is pleasing **to him**)
*A los alumnos **les** gustan las matemáticas*　(literally: **to** the pupils, maths is pleasing **to them**).

2. If we are referring to a pronoun, and want to make clear whether the person we are referring to is masculine or feminine, we must insert "*a*" before the appropriate personal pronoun, and then use the indirect pronoun *le* (singular) or *les* (plural) as above.

*A **él** le gusta la música*　　　　　(literally: **to he**, music is pleasing to him)
*A **ella** le gusta la música*　　　　(literally: **to she**, music is pleasing to her)
*A **ellos** les gusta la música*　　　(literally: **to they**, music is pleasing to them)
*A **ellas** les gusta la música*　　　(literally: **to they**, music is pleasing to them)

Note also:
*A **Vd.** le gusta la música*　　　　(literally: **to your honour**, music is pleasing to him)
*A **Vds.** les gusta la música*　　　(literally: **to your honours**, music is pleasing to them)

Finally, please note that with *gustar* one always uses the definite article when saying what one likes. One likes *the* music, or *the* maths, etc.

Exercise 3.5

¡Escucha y escribe!
Completa las frases y escribe en inglés

1. *¡Hola! Me llamo Enrique. Me ___ los deportes.*
2. *Buenos días. Me llamo Helena. ___ el alemán.*
3. *¡Hola! ¿___? Me gustan ___ .*
4. *Ana estudia la química pero ___.*
5. *¡Muy buenas! Me llamo ___. Me ___ las ciencias pero no ___.*

Exercice 3.6

¡Habla!
Habla con tu amigo de las asignaturas que te gustan y de las asignaturas que no te gustan.

Ejemplo: ¿Qué asignaturas te gustan?
Me gustan la religión y las matemáticas.

Exercice 3.7

¡Escribe!
¿Cómo se escribe en español?

1. I like school.
2. I don't like the homework.
3. I like languages.
4. I don't like maths.
5. What subject do you like? (Familiar, singular)
6. You like history and geography, don't you? (Polite, singular)
7. He likes art.
8. She likes sport.
9. Which subjects do you like? (Polite, plural)
10. We don't like science because we don't like the teacher.
11. Pupils, what subjects do you like? (Familiar, plural)
12. They like computer studies, but they don't like Religious Studies.

Exercise 3.8

¡Escribe en inglés!

1. *No comemos paella.*
2. *No bebemos coca cola en la cantina.*
3. *No me gusta la química.*
4. *No trabajo en mi casa.*
5. *Mis amigos fuman en la biblioteca.*
6. *A Vds. les gusta el colegio, ¿verdad?*
7. *No tengo mi cuaderno.*
8. *No vivimos en Barcelona.*
9. *Mis padres no son de Irlanda.*
10. *No tengo 15 años.*

Exercise 3.9 🕮

¡Escucha y rellena la ficha!

Nombre	☺ Le gusta(n)	☹ No le gusta(n)
Enrique	la informática	el dibujo
Helena		
Ana		
Verónica		
Alberto		

Note that when Alberto told us what he does and doesn't like, he added two little words: *me gusta **mucho** y no me gusta **nada.*** These phrases can be translated as "I really like" and "I don't like …. at all".

Exercise 3.10 ✍

¡Escribe en español!

1. I don't study Latin at all.
2. We don't live in Spain.
3. My sister does not study much.
4. I'm not learning German.
5. We don't speak French at all.
6. I really like History.
7. My headmaster is very annoying.
8. My brother really likes Mathematics.
9. My friends do not like sport at all.
10. I really don't like science.

¿Qué piensas?

We are now going to learn how to broaden our answers to questions about a range of school subjects! *¡Escucha y lee!*:

- *Estudio muchas asignaturas. Me gusta el español pero prefiero la historia. Pienso que es muy interesante.*

- *No me gusta nada la geografía. Pienso que es muy aburrida.*

- *Yo prefiero el inglés. Pienso que las clases son muy interesantes y me llevo bien con el profesor.*

Notice how the ability to give an opinion allows us to give a much fuller answer than previously. From now on, then, **never** give one-word answers when you can expand these into a couple of sentences which include your opinion. To vary the way you do this, here are some more verbs and phrases you can use:

Creo que
Pienso que } = I think
Opino que

En mi opinión = In my opinion
A mi juicio = In my judgement

N.B. when you use *creo que, pienso que* and *opino que*, **you must include the *que*.** We don't always include the word "that" in English: I think the book is brilliant or I think **that** the book is brilliant are both correct. But in Spanish, we **must use *que*.**

E.g. *Creo **que** el libro es interesante.*

Exercise 3.11

¡Escucha!

Listen to the following students giving their opinions on the subjects that they study. Pay attention to how they give their opinions. Make a note in Spanish about what they say.

1. Marisa
2. Félix
3. Manuel

4. Begoña
5. Harold

E.C.A*

When giving a response, either written or verbal, to a question, it is always a good idea to write or say as much as you can. Trust me. So we're now going to play the E.C.A* game. You're probably aware that an A* is the highest grade at GCSE, and in exams it is always a good idea to aim for the top grade. This game will get you into good habits. It works like this:

¿Quieres aprender español?

E grade answer: *Sí.*

C grade answer: *Sí, quiero aprender español.*

A* grade answer: *Sí, quiero aprender español porque es muy interesante. Creo que es una asignatura muy útil y me llevo bien con mi profesor – ¡es estupendo!*

What have we achieved in this last answer? We have expanded our basic answer by giving a **reason** and an **opinion** and these, with **accuracy**, are a hallmark of a good grade in this subject. Believe me. It also allows you to practise speaking as much Spanish as you can. Practice makes perfect, remember. (It will also mean that your teacher will have to do more marking!)

Exercise 3.12

¡Habla y escribe!

Write or say three answers to the following questions, using first an E grade answer, then a C grade answer, and finally an A* grade answer.

1. *¿Te gusta el colegio?*
2. *¿Son simpáticos tus profesores?*
3. *¿Te gusta la Navidad?*

Exercise 3.13

¡Habla!

Habla con tu amigo de las asignaturas que te gustan y por qué te gustan.
Ahora habla con tu amigo de las asignaturas que no te gustan.
Remember to give reasons!

Radical changing verbs: e → ie

Now for a challenge as we face radical changing verbs! We have already learnt quite a lot about Spanish verbs. There are regular verbs (*hablar, comer, vivir*) and irregular verbs (*ser, tener*). Well this next group consists of verbs which are regular with regard to their **endings** but which undergo a change in their **stem** on the stressed vowel.

The first type we are going to meet are DOUBLE VOWEL CHANGE verbs. With these verbs, **E** changes to **IE** in those forms where the *E* is being stressed. Luckily, this is always in the same place with every verb, so it is very easy to learn the pattern. Radical changing verbs may be *AR*, *ER* or *IR*:

Pensar (ie) = to think

AR		
	pienso	pensamos
	piensas	pensáis
	piensa	piensan

Querer (ie) = to want

ER		
	quiero	queremos
	quieres	queréis
	quiere	quieren

Preferir (ie) = to prefer

IR		
	prefiero	preferimos
	prefieres	preferís
	prefiere	prefieren

Note how the **endings** are regular, but the *e* in the **stem** changes to *ie* in four of the persons: 1st, 2nd and 3rd singular, and 3rd plural. There is no way of predicting whether a verb will be radical changing or not – you'll just have to learn them as you meet them! But if they *are* radical changing, you will find them written with (*ie*) after the verb, like this: *pensar (ie)*.

You will meet other types of radical changing verbs later, but this should do for now.

Exercise 3.14

¡Escribe en español!
Write out in full the present tense of the following verbs:

1. *Fregar (ie)* = to scrub, wash (e.g. the dishes)
2. *Perder (ie)* = to lose
3. *Mentir (ie)* = to tell a lie

Exercise 3.15

¿Cómo se dice en español?

1. Do you prefer Spanish or German?
2. She thinks that History is interesting.
3. They prefer Science because they think that it is easy.
4. Why do you want to work at home?
5. We think that the teachers in our school prefer to teach the older pupils.

Ermenegildo friega los platos

La hora
¡Mira y escucha!

El reloj = the clock, watch

A la una – at one o'clock

A las dos – at two o'clock

A las tres – at three o'clock

A las cuatro – at four o'clock

A las cinco – at five o'clock

A las seis – at six o'clock

A las siete – at seven o'clock

A las ocho – at eight o'clock

A las nueve – at nine o'clock

A las diez – at ten o'clock

A las once – at eleven o'clock

A las doce – at twelve o'clock

¿Qué hora es?

To say that the time is something **o'clock**,
we use **es** for one o'clock (because one is singular) and **son** for all the other hours (which are plural).

E.g. *Es la una* = it is one o'clock.
E.g. *Son las dos* = it is two o'clock.
E.g. *Son las tres* = it is three o'clock.

To be precise, we can add *en punto* (= o'clock, on the dot).

To say **quarter past**, we add **y cuarto**.
E.g. *Es la una y cuarto* = it is quarter past one (literally: one o'clock and a quarter).

To say **half past**, we add **y media**.
E.g. *Son las cuatro y media* = it is half past four (literally: four o'clock and a half).

To say **quarter to**, we use **menos cuarto**.
E.g. *Son las nueve menos cuarto* = it is quarter to nine (literally: nine o'clock minus a quarter).

Exercise 3.16
¡Habla y escribe!
Give the time as shown on the following clocks:

1.

2.

3.

4.

5.

6.

7.

8.

9.

10.

Exercise 3.17

¡Escribe la hora!

1. *Son las dos menos cuarto.*
2. *Es la una y media.*
3. *Son las siete.*
4. *Son las cinco y cuarto.*
5. *Son las cuatro y cuarto.*

6. *Son las once y media.*
7. *Son las doce menos cuarto.*
8. *Son las tres.*
9. *Son las dos y media.*
10. *Son las cuatro.*

Exercise 3.18

¡Habla!

Take out a copy of your school timetable and, in pairs, ask and answer the following questions.

1. *¿A qué hora llegas al colegio?*
2. *¿Cuántas clases de historia tienes?*
3. *¿Cuántas clases de inglés tienes?*
4. *¿Cuántas clases de geografía tienes?*

5. *¿Cuándo tienes historia?*
6. *¿A qué hora tienes inglés?*
7. *¿Dónde y cuándo tienes geografía?*
8. *¿En qué aula tienes ciencias?*

Empezar (ie) y comenzar (ie)

Now for two more radical changing verbs: *empezar (ie)* and *comenzar (ie)* which both mean "to begin". They work in exactly the same way as the other radical changing verbs you have met, and to prove it, here they are in full:

Empezar (ie)

empiezo   *empezamos*
empiezas   *empezáis*
empieza   *empiezan*

Comenzar (ie)

comienzo   *comenzamos*
comienzas   *comenzáis*
comienza   *comienzan*

These two are obviously quite useful verbs now that we are talking about the time.

E.g. *¿A qué hora empiezan tus clases?*
Mis clases empiezan a las nueve.
¿A qué hora comienza tu clase de historia?
Mi clase de historia comienza a las dos.

Exercise 3.19

¡Escribe y habla !
Escribe tu horario y contesta las preguntas:

1. *¿A qué hora empieza tu próxima clase de español?*
2. *¿A qué hora empieza tu próxima clase de inglés?*
3. *¿A qué hora empieza tu próxima clase de matemáticas?*
4. *¿A qué hora empieza tu próxima clase de francés?*
5. *¿A qué hora empieza tu próxima clase de deportes?*
6. *¿A qué hora empieza tu próxima clase de historia?*

Hacer

The verb *hacer* = "to do" or "to make" is one of the most important verbs in the Spanish language. It is irregular in the first person singular (where a *g* creeps in, quite uninvited!).

ha**go**	hacemos
haces	hacéis
hace	hacen

Exercise 3.20

¡Escribe en inglés!

1. *¿Qué haces a las nueve?*
   Llego al colegio.

2. *¿Qué haces a las diez?*
   Aprendo español.

3. *¿Qué haces a las once?*
   Tengo un recreo.

4. *¿Qué hacéis a la una?*
   ¡Comemos!

Exercise 3.21

¡Escribe en español las preguntas y contesta!
1. What do you do at school on Mondays?
2. What do we do today after lunch?
3. What do you do at home after school?
4. What do the teachers do at three thirty today?
5. What do we do after lunch on Fridays?

Exercise 3.22

¡Habla!

Answer the following questions as fully as you can in Spanish and give your opinion whenever you can. Work in pairs or groups.

1. *¿Cuántas asignaturas estudias en el colegio?*
2. *¿Cuántas asignaturas son obligatorias?*
3. *¿Cuáles son las asignaturas optativas?*
4. *¿A qué hora empiezan las clases?*
5. *¿Hay recreo? ¿A qué hora? ¿Qué haces durante el recreo?*
6. *¿A qué hora comes?*
7. *¿Cuál es tu asignatura preferida? ¿Por qué?*
8. *¿Qué asignatura no te gusta? ¿Por qué?*
9. *¿A qué hora termina el colegio?*
10. *¿Te gusta tu colegio? ¿Por qué?*

> **Vocabulario**
> *Obligatorio* = compulsory
> *Optativo* = optional
> *El recreo* = the break

Exercise 3.23

¡Escribe!

Now write an article for your Spanish friend's school magazine telling him/her about your school. Don't forget to include:

- What time school starts
- What you do every day
- Which subjects you do
- Those which you like
- Those which you do not like
- Those which you prefer

And most importantly: **Give your opinions**!

Exercise 3.24

¡Lee y escucha!

MI HORARIO

¡Hola! Soy Eduardo Hernández. Tengo dieciséis años y estoy en el 4° año de Educación Secundaria Obligatoria en la Academia Santa Teresa en Málaga.

Os voy a hablar sobre mi horario. Tengo clases desde las 8.15 hasta las 2.30, de lunes a viernes. Hay un recreo de media hora a las 12.30 en el que solemos tomar un bocadillo o un donut y charlar con los amigos. Cada clase dura 55 minutos – mucho, ¿verdad?

*Estudio muchas asignaturas: tengo 4 clases de lengua española, matemáticas e inglés por semana; 3 clases de geografía, historia, física, química e informática. Tengo también 2 clases de ética, y 1 clase de religión, dibujo y educación física. Normalmente hacemos gimnasia pero a veces jugamos al balonmano, baloncesto y fútbol sala (5 personas por equipo). ¡Ah, se me olvidaba, una vez por semana tengo una hora de tutoría! Lo bueno es que no hay clases por la tarde pero lo malo es que hay deberes **todos los días** – ¡qué pesado!*

¿Qué os parece mi horario? ¿Vosotros tenéis que trabajar tanto?

<table>
<tr><td>Vocabulario</td></tr>
</table>

4° = cuarto (equivalent to year 11)
Educación Secundaria
    Obligatoria = Secondary School
Sobre = about
Desde = from
Hasta = until
Solemos = we usually...
Un bocadillo = a sandwich
Charlar = to chat

E = and

Ética = ethics

A veces = sometimes
Balonmano = handball
Baloncesto = basketball
Fútbol sala = indoor football
Olvidar = to forget
Una vez = one time
La tarde = the afternoon/evening
¡Qué pesado! = what a pain!
¿Qué os parece? = what do you
    think?

N.B.
1° ESO = year 8
2° ESO = year 9
3° ESO = year 10
4° ESO = year 11
Cursar 4° de ESO = to be in
    year 11

1. *¿Dónde estudia Eduardo?*
2. *¿En qué curso está?* (*el curso* = school year)
3. *¿A qué hora empiezan las clases y a qué hora terminan?*
4. *¿Tiene colegio los sábados?*
5. *¿Cuándo es el recreo? Y ¿qué hacen durante el recreo?*
6. *¿Cuánto tiempo dura cada clase?*
7. *¿Cuántas clases por semana tiene de inglés y de física?*
8. *¿Qué deportes practica en el colegio?*
9. *¿Qué es lo malo de su colegio?*
10. *¿Qué es lo bueno?*

Y and e

N.B. The conjunction *e* = 'and' is used instead of *y* before words beginning with *i* and *hi* (but not, just to keep you on your toes, *hie*).

E.g.   *Matemáticas **e** inglés **e** historia.*

Vocabulario 3.1

Aburrido = boring
Divertido = funny/amusing
Fácil = easy
Interesante = interesting
Preferido = favourite
Útil = useful

Durar = to last
Empezar (ie) = to begin
Explicar = to explain
Gustar = to please
Me llevo bien con = I get on well with
Pensar (ie) = to think
Preferir (ie) = to prefer
Se me da bien = I'm good at
Se me da fatal = I'm bad at

El almuerzo = the lunch
El director = the headmaster
El horario = timetable
El reloj = clock, watch
La asignatura = subject
Los deberes = homework
Lo bueno = the good thing
Lo malo = the bad thing

De media = on average
Desde = from
Hasta = until
¿Por qué? = why
Porque = because
Sobre = about
E = and

Exercise 3.25

Repaso

You have now learnt how all three types of regular verbs work, as well as a number of irregular verbs and some radical changing verbs. Here's your opportunity to show off your skill. Conjugate (i.e. write out in full) and give the meanings of the following verbs:

1.   *Practicar*
2.   *Escribir*
3.   *Comer*
4.   *Tener*
5.   *Preferir (ie)*
6.   *Pensar (ie)*
7.   *Vender*
8.   *Decidir*
9.   *Escuchar*
10. *Ser*
11. *Hacer*
12. *Hablar*

Now make a display showing the three types of regular verbs (*AR*, *ER* and *IR*), together with the irregular verbs you have learnt. Think of a way of showing how radical changing verbs can be displayed. Highlight the endings carefully to show how regular verbs fit into groups and behave in a way that can be predicted, and how irregular ones just have to be learnt.

La comida y la bebida

El desayuno

A typical breakfast in Spain might comprise:

- *el café / el café con leche* = coffee / coffee with milk

- *el zumo de naranja* = orange juice

- *el jamón* = ham

- *el queso* = cheese

- *el yogur* = yoghurt

- *las tostadas* = toast

La comida

In Spain the mid-day meal, *la comida* or *el almuerzo*, is generally taken between 2.00 and 4.00 p.m., somewhat later than in the UK. It is after this meal that *¡Buenos días!* becomes *¡Buenas tardes!* It is also the time, especially in the south of the country and particularly in summer, that the Spanish take their *siesta* or afternoon nap.

- *la sopa* = soup

- *la ensalada* = salad

- *la tortilla* = omelette

- *la pasta* = pasta

- *el jamón* = ham

- *el postre* = dessert

- *el queso* = cheese

- *el pescado* = fish

- *el vino (tinto, blanco o rosado)* = wine (red, white or rosé)

- *el pan* = bread

- *el agua* mineral (con gas / sin gas)* = mineral water (fizzy / still)

- *el cocido* = stew

- *las patatas* = potatoes

***N.B.** If a feminine noun begins with a stressed *a,* although it is feminine, the article *el* is used, to make the word easier to say. E.g. *el agua* is feminine.

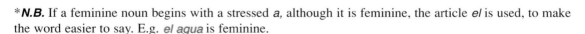

En España
Pasta is the slang term for cash!

La merienda
A snack often comes in handy at around 5.00 or 6.00 p.m., as people eat quite late in Spain.

- *el bocadillo (el bocata) con chocolate* = baguette with chocolate

- *el bollo* = bun

- *el chorizo o salchichón* = red sausage or salami

- *el donut* = donut

- *las galletas* = biscuits

- *el batido* = milkshake in carton

La cena
The evening meal tends to happen after about 9.00 p.m., the time at which *¡Buenas tardes!* becomes *¡Buenas noches!*, although this is obviously by no means an exact science! A typical menu might include:

- *el pollo* = chicken

- *la ternera* = beef

- *el cordero* = lamb

- *el cerdo* = pork

La bebida
Beer, *la cerveza*, is very popular in Spain, the most famous brands being *San Miguel, Cruzcampo* and *Aguila Amstel*, although imported beers such as Heineken are also common. *Una clara* (shandy) is a refreshing solution on a hot day as are *los refrescos* (soft-drinks) such as *Coca Cola, Fanta naranja* and *Fanta limón*.

However, of all drinks, Spain is probably most famous for one called *Sangría*, a mixture of spirits, red and white wine, fruit juice and fruit.

En España
Paella is one of Spain's national dishes and originates from Valencia. It is a rice dish traditionally with rabbit, chicken and lots of seafood and vegetables and it takes its name from the big round pan in which it is cooked.

Exercise 3.26

¡Lee y escucha!

LA FAMILIA HERNÁNDEZ

La familia Hernández es una familia típica española. Viven en Madrid.

Por la mañana, para desayunar, los señores Hernández normalmente beben café con leche, pero a sus tres hijos no les gusta. Pablo, el mayor, toma un vaso de leche caliente, mientras que sus hermanos menores, Eduardo y Mari Carmen, prefieren tomar Colacao. Los padres comen pan tostado con un poco de queso y jamón. Sus hijos prefieren galletas María, donuts o algunas veces un yogur. No suelen tomar cereales para el desayuno como en Inglaterra.

A las dos y pico, el señor Hernández vuelve a casa para comer porque trabaja cerca en una oficina. Su mujer es ama de casa y por eso prepara la comida para su familia. Pablo no regresa a casa para comer porque estudia en la Universidad. Eduardo y Mari Carmen sí vuelven para almorzar porque su colegio está cerca.

De primer plato casi siempre toman sopa (sobre todo en invierno) o una ensalada o verduras, o a veces una tortilla española.

De segundo comen carne – pollo con patatas fritas o filetes de ternera – o pescado – merluza, lenguado o mariscos. A veces la madre prepara un cocido muy sabroso con garbanzos – ¡el famoso cocido madrileño!, que les gusta mucho. Siempre comen pan con la comida y suelen beber agua mineral sin gas. Los padres toman también vino tinto o blanco. De postre normalmente toman fruta, flan o en verano algunas veces helado.

Después de la comida, sobre las 3, el señor Hernández tiene que volver a la oficina y sus dos hijos menores al colegio. A las 6 Eduardo y Mari Carmen regresan a casa (con bastante hambre) y toman la merienda – normalmente un vaso de Nesquik o leche con un bollo o pan con nocilla.

La cena empieza a eso de las 9 y consiste en algo más ligero que la comida – a veces una tortilla francesa, algo de pasta, o quizás un poco de pescado o verduras, queso o jamón. A la familia Hernández no les gusta cenar mucho de noche, porque no es sano.

Note how *sí* may be used for emphasis:

Eduardo y Marie Carmen sí vuelven = Eduardo and Marie Carmen *do* return.

Vocabulario

Desayunar = to have breakfast
Un vaso = a glass
Caliente = hot
Mientras = while
Un poco = a little
Las galletas = biscuits
Algunas veces = sometimes
A las dos y pico = at around 2 o'clock
Vuelve = (he) returns
Cerca = close, near
El ama (f.) *de casa* = housewife
Casi = almost
Sobre todo = especially
Las verduras = vegetables
La merluza = hake (a type of stew)
El lenguado = sole
Los mariscos = sea-food
Sabroso = flavoursome
Los garbanzos = chickpeas

Suelen = they usually...

El helado = ice-cream

El hambre (f.) = hunger

La nocilla = chocolate spread

A eso de = at around
Algo = something
Ligero = light
Sano = healthy

Ejercicio A

Subraya la respuesta correcta, como en el ejemplo:

1. La familia Hernández es una típica familia:
   a) *mejicana*
   b) *italiana*
   c) *española*

2. Para el desayuno toman:
   a) *café con leche*
   b) *leche*
   c) *café con leche, leche y Colacao.*

3. Los padres desayunan :
   a) *cereales*
   b) *yogur*
   c) *tostadas*

4. Comen a las dos:
   a) *en punto*
   b) *y pico*
   c) *y cinco*

Ejercicio B

¿Verdad o mentira? Escribe ✓ o ✗ al final de cada frase, como en el ejemplo:

1. Mari Carmen prepara la comida. ✗

2. Toda la familia come en casa.

3. De primer plato normalmente toman sopa o ensalada.

4. De segundo solo comen carne.

5. El cocido es un plato típico de Barcelona.

6. Todos beben vino con la comida.

Ejercicio C

Contesta las preguntas, como en el ejemplo;

1. ¿Cuál es el postre normalmente?
   Normalmente el postre es fruta, flan o helado.

2. ¿Qué comen siempre con la comida?

3. ¿Qué beben?

4. ¿A qué hora meriendan Eduardo y Mari Carmen?

5. ¿Qué toman para la merienda?

6. ¿Cuándo cenan?

7. ¿En qué consiste la cena?

8. ¿Por qué no cenan mucho?

Exercise 3.27

¡Habla!

1. ¿A qué hora desayunas?

2. ¿Qué tomas para el desayuno? ¿Qué bebes?

3. ¿Cuándo tomas el almuerzo?

4. ¿Cuál es tu comida preferida?

5. ¿Cuál es tu bebida preferida?

Exercise 3.28

¡Lee y escucha!
José y Cristina hacen una encuesta sobre la comida en su colegio.

José: *¡Hola! Cristina y yo hacemos una encuesta sobre la comida en nuestro colegio. Queremos saber cuántos alumnos comen en el cole, cuáles son sus comidas favoritas, qué beben normalmente, cuánto tiempo dura el almuerzo, y qué piensan de la comida.*

Cristina: *Sí, y también queremos saber qué comen en casa. Pensamos que todo el mundo debería tener una dieta equilibrada y queremos saber si las comidas en este colegio son sanas.*

José: *Empezamos con los alumnos más jóvenes de nuestro colegio. Éste es Juan...*

Cristina: *Y ésta es Teresa. Así que Teresa, ¿qué tal?*

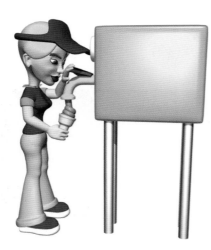

Teresa: *Muy bien, gracias. ¿Y tú?*

Cristina: *Estupendo, gracias. Así que ¿cuál es la hora de comer?*

Teresa: *Sí, comemos a la una y media. Tenemos cuarenta y cinco minutos para el almuerzo.*

Cristina: *¿Qué tomas hoy, Juan?*

Juan: *Hoy tomo cocido con patatas y verduras. Bebo agua; ¡sólo hay agua en el cole!*

Cristina: *¿Cuál es tu comida favorita, Teresa?*

Teresa: *Mi comida favorita es la paella pero me gusta también el pescado y me encanta la pizza.*

Cristina: *Gracias, Teresa. Gracias, Juan. ¡Que aproveche!*

Vocabulario

Hacer una encuesta = to conduct a survey

Saber = to know

durar = to last

Todo el mundo = everybody
Debería (conditional) = ought
Una dieta equilibrada = a balanced diet

Joven = young

¡Que aproveche! = enjoy your meal

¡Contesta las preguntas!

1.   *¿Qué tipo de encuesta es?*
2.   *¿Por qué es importante según Cristina?*
3.   *¿Quiénes son los primeros alumnos a quienes entrevistan José y Cristina?*
4.   *¿A qué hora comen los alumnos?*
5.   *¿Cuánto tiempo tienen para comer?*
6.   *Describe lo que come Juan.*
7.   *¿Cuál es la comida favorita de Teresa? Y ¿cuáles son las otras comidas que menciona?*
8.   *¿Qué dice Cristina al final de la entrevista?*

Possessive adjectives

We have already learnt how to say my, your and his. So now we can learn how to say our, your and their.

Singular		Plural		
Masculine	**Feminine**	**Masculine**	**Feminine**	
mi	*mi*	*mis*	*mis*	My
tu	*tu*	*tus*	*tus*	Your
su	*su*	*sus*	*sus*	His/her
nuestro	*nuestra*	*nuestros*	*nuestras*	Our
vuestro	*vuestra*	*vuestros*	*vuestras*	Your
su	*su*	*sus*	*sus*	Their

Demonstrative pronouns

And we should also explain some other little chaps which are popping up now and again, namely the demonstrative pronouns *éste, ésta* and *esto*. These words all mean "this" and are used to point out someone or something. For masculine nouns we use *éste;* for feminine nouns we use *ésta;* and if we are referring to a noun with no obvious gender, we use *esto*.

E.g. **Éste** *es Juan ...*   **ésta** *es Cristina ...*   *pero ¿qué es* **esto***?*

Exercise 3.29

¡Lee y escucha!

José: *Hola, Cristina y yo hacemos una encuesta en nuestro colegio. ¿Cómo te llamas?*

Eduardo: *Yo me llamo Eduardo. Soy nuevo en el colegio. Estoy en el segundo año de Educación Secundaria Obligatoria. Ésta es mi amiga Elena.*

José: *¿Qué piensas de la comida aquí?*

Eduardo: *¡Es horrible! y no hay suficiente para elegir.*

Elena: *Él es muy especial para la comida. La comida está bien. A mí me chifla el cocido, y las pizzas, claro.*

José: *¿Cuál es tu comida favorita?*

Elena: *Es el cochinillo, pero no lo comemos nunca en el cole. Lo tomamos en casa y está riquísimo.*

José: *¿Y tú, Eduardo? ¿Qué comida te gusta más?*

Eduardo: *¿A mí? Pues, me gusta el pollo al ajillo y los calamares a la romana. Mi abuela los cocina muy bien el fin de semana. ¡Es una cocinera fantástica!*

Vocabulario

Nuevo = new

Elegir = to choose
Especial = fussy
Me chifla = I love

El cochinillo = suckling pig
Nunca = never
Riquísimo = delicious

Pues = well...um...
El pollo al ajillo = chicken cooked in garlic
Los calamares a la romana = squid cooked in batter
La cocinera = cook (f)

Contesta las preguntas

1. *¿Quién es Eduardo? Y ¿en qué clase está?*
2. *¿Quién es Elena?*
3. *¿Qué opina Eduardo de la comida del colegio?*
4. *¿Por qué piensa así?*
5. *¿Elena opina como Eduardo?*
6. *¿Qué comidas del colegio menciona Elena?*
7. *¿Cuál es su comida preferida? ¿Dónde come?*
8. *¿Cuál es la comida favorita de Eduardo? Y ¿Quién se la prepara?*

Vocabulario 3.2

Cenar = to have supper
Cocinar = to cook
Consistir en = to consist of
Desayunar = to have breakfast
Me chifla (like gustar) = I love/I'm mad about

El agua (fem.) = water
El bollo = bun/cake
El cocinero = cook
El vaso = glass
La cena = dinner
La comida = food, lunch
Las patatas fritas = chips

Nuevo = new
Riquísimo = delicious
Sabroso = tasty
Sano = healthy

Lo = it (direct pronoun)
Los = them (direct pronoun)

Algunas veces = sometimes
Así = like that
De primer plato = as a first course
De segundo = as the main course
Mientras que = whereas
Pues = well, um...

Deberes

¡Investiga!

Choose one of the major regions of Spain and, using the internet or other resources in the library, draw up a menu for a Spanish restaurant, selecting specialities from the region you have chosen and pricing each dish appropriately. Do the same for the wine list, again (where possible) selecting wines from different regions.

Expectations

At the end of this unit

You should be able to: make statements and ask questions about which subjects you like, dislike and prefer; understand and use radical-changing verbs; identify a radical-changing verb from its dictionary entry; describe your timetable and give times in response to questions such as ¿*Qué haces a las ... ?*; describe your school, and say how many teachers and pupils it has; describe and ask questions about mealtimes.

You may also be able to: express opinions by saying why you like or dislike something, using *pensar* and adjectives; write compound sentences, largely from memory, describing your school day and mealtimes; use a dictionary or glossary to find the words you need.

About the unit

In this unit you learn to ask and answer questions about daily routines and where you live. You describe what you and others do. You begin to develop creative writing skills.

New contexts:

- daily routine
- simple descriptions of homes

New language content:

- reflexive verbs
- radical changing verbs *o → ue*
- both verbs meaning 'to be': *ser* and *estar*
- numbers above 100
- ordinal numbers
- prepositions

La rutina diaria

In this unit we learn how to describe our homes and our daily routine. First we need to learn more about radical changing verbs, then we need to learn about reflexive verbs; so brace yourselves!

More on radical changing verbs: o > ue

So far we have met just one type of radical changing verb: the double vowel change verbs which see the letter *e* change to *ie* in the stressed forms. A second type of double vowel change verb is where the letter **o** changes to **ue**. This occurs in verbs of all three types (*AR*, *ER* and *IR*), for example *almorzar (ue)*, *volver (ue)* and *dormir (ue)*. The change occurs in the usual places (i.e. all except 1st and 2nd person plural), and again, you just have to learn that a verb will behave like this when you first meet it. The (*ue*) tells you that it is such a verb.

AR   **almorzar (ue)** = to have lunch

	Singular	Plural
1st person	almuerzo	almorzamos
2nd person	almuerzas	almorzáis
3rd person	almuerza	almuerzan

ER   **volver (ue)** = to return

	Singular	Plural
1st person	vuelvo	volvemos
2nd person	vuelves	volvéis
3rd person	vuelve	vuelven

IR   **dormir (ue)** = to sleep

	Singular	Plural
1st person	duermo	dormimos
2nd person	duermes	dormís
3rd person	duerme	duermen

Exercise 4.1

¿Cómo se dice en español?

1. We sleep in the classroom!
2. They have lunch at one o'clock.
3. I return from school at half past four.
4. My friends and I have lunch in the canteen.
5. My teacher returns to Extremadura each year.
6. I sleep until 11 o'clock on Sundays.

Exercise 4.2

¡Escribe!

Write out in full the following verbs:

1. *Soler (ue)* = to be accustomed to
2. *Jugar (ue)* = to play
3. *Encontrar (ue)* = to meet, to find
4. *Torcer (ue)* = to twist, to turn

Los verbos reflexivos

We have already met reflexive pronouns in phrases such as *¿Cómo te llamas?* and *me llamo*. We are now going to see how these work in more detail.

A reflexive verb describes an action that one does to oneself. Thus *me llamo* literally means **I call myself.** The word *me* is a reflexive pronoun, meaning "myself", and *llamo* is a verb meaning "I call".

To be able to deal with a reflexive verb, then, you need to learn the reflexive pronouns, both singular and plural:

		Singular		**Plural**	
1st person	*Me*	= myself	*Nos*	= ourselves	
2nd person	*Te*	= yourself	*Os*	= yourselves	
3rd person	*Se*	= himself, herself, itself	*Se*	= themselves.	

As you can see, these are almost identical to the indirect pronouns you met in Unit 3. Only in the 3rd person is there any difference. And here they are in action:

1st person	*Me llamo*	I am called	*Nos llamamos*	We are called
2nd person	*Te llamas*	You are called	*Os llamáis*	You are called
3rd person	*Se llama*	He/she/it is called	*Se llaman*	They are called

As always, the 3rd person forms are used with *Vd.* and *Vds.*
E.g. *¿Cómo **se** llama Vd.?*
        *¿Cómo **se** llaman Vds.?*

The infinitive of the verb 'to call oneself' is *llamarse*. You can tell if a verb is reflexive as the infinitive will end in *-arse*, *-erse* or *-irse*: the *-se* bit denotes that it's reflexive and the *-ar*, *-er* or *-ir* bit tells you which type of verb it is (*-AR*, *-ER* or *-IR*).

Exercise 4.3

¡Escribe!
1.   Write out in full the following verbs:
       (a) *levantarse* = to get up
       (b) *bañarse*   = to have a bath
       (c) *lavarse*   = to have a wash
       (d) *ducharse* = to have a shower

2.   Write a series of brief sentences using each of the verbs in the vocabulary below:

Ejemplo: El chico se levanta a las siete =
             the boy gets up at 7 o'clock.

Vocabulario	
Levantarse	To get up
Lavarse	To have a wash
Ducharse	To have a shower
Peinarse	To comb one's hair
Limpiarse los dientes	To brush one's teeth
Quitarse la ropa	To get undressed
Bañarse	To have a bath, to bathe

Exercise 4.4

¡Lee o escucha!
Read or listen to the following passage and then match up 1 – 6 with A – H.

Me llamo Juan y me despierto a las siete. Me levanto normalmente a las siete y media. Después de levantarme, me ducho en el cuarto de baño. Después de vestirme, tomo el desayuno en el comedor. Mi hermana se levanta a las siete. No se ducha normalmente pero se lava el pelo cada mañana. Mis padres son muy perezosos ¡Siempre se levantan a las ocho y media! Por la tarde me acuesto bastante tarde a las once y media.

1.	*Juan se levanta*	a)	*a las dos*
2.	*En el cuarto de baño*	b)	*a las ocho y media*
3.	*Su hermana se levanta*	c)	*a las seis*
4.	*Se lava el pelo*	d)	*a las once y media*
5.	*Los padres de Juan se levantan*	e)	*cada mañana*
6.	*Juan se acuesta*	f)	*a las siete*
		g)	*se ducha*
		h)	*nunca*
		i)	*a las siete y media*

Radical changing reflexives!

Just to increase the fun, a reflexive verb can be radical vowel changing. For example the verb *despertarse (ie)* that we met above is both reflexive and radical vowel changing. And such verbs can be (*ue*) or (*ie*). Thus we get verbs going like this:

*Acostarse (**ue**) = to go to bed*	
me acuesto	*nos acostamos*
te acuestas	*os acostáis*
se acuesta	*se acuestan*

*Despertarse (**ie**) = to wake up*	
me despierto	*nos despertamos*
te despiertas	*os despertáis*
se despierta	*se despiertan*

Exercise 4.5

¡Escribe en inglés!
1. *Me acuesto a las diez normalmente.*
2. *Sus amigos se llaman Pedro y Juan.*
3. *Nos levantamos tarde los domingos.*
4. *¡Mi hermano no se lava!*
5. *Te limpias los dientes en el cuarto de baño.*

Exercise 4.6

¡Escribe en español!
1. I have a shower every morning.
2. I wash my hair on Tuesdays and Fridays.
3. She wakes up at half past six.
4. They get undressed in their bedroom.
5. You (polite, plural form) go to bed quite late.

Single vowel change radical changing verbs

The last type of radical changing verb that we must look at is called **a single vowel change verb**. With these verbs, as the name suggests, there is a *single* vowel change, from *E* to *I*, and only IR Verbs can fall into this category.

Seguir (i) = to follow	
Sigo*	Seguimos
Sigues	Seguís
Sigue	Siguen

Vestirse (i) = to get dressed	
Me visto	Nos vestimos
Te vistes	Os vestís
Se viste	Se visten

*__N.B.__ Just to be difficult, *seguir* drops its *u* in the 1st person singular.

Exercise 4.7

¡Escucha!

Corrige las frases siguientes / Correct the following sentences

E.g.   *El chico se llama ~~Juan~~*
        El chico se llama Julián

1.   *Julián se levanta a las seis.*
2.   *Se levanta en el cuarto de baño.*
3.   *Se viste después de tomar el desayuno.*
4.   *Le gusta el café con leche.*
5.   *Se lava los dientes antes de tomar el desayuno.*
6.   *Coge el autobús para llegar al instituto.*
7.   *El viaje dura 2 minutos.*
8.   *Almuerza en su casa.*
9.   *Hace sus deberes por la noche.*
10. *Vuelve a su casa a las siete.*

Exercise 4.8

¡Habla!

Pregunta a tu pareja:

1.   *¿A qué hora te despiertas por la mañana?*
2.   *¿Dónde te vistes?*
3.   *¿Te duchas o te bañas por la mañana?*
4.   *¿Qué haces después de vestirte?*
5.   *¿Qué tomas para el desayuno?*
6.   *¿Qué haces antes de salir para ir al colegio?*

Soler (ue)

Soler + the infinitive = to be accustomed to do something and is a handy expression to use in Spanish. Although 'to be accustomed' sounds rather formal, we can translate it into English as 'normally' + verb.

E.g.   *Suelo comer paella* = I normally eat paella.

E.g.   *Suelo aprender el vocabulario* = I normally learn my vocabulary.

Here's the verb in full:

	Singular	Plural
1st person	Suelo	Solemos
2nd person	Sueles	Soléis
3rd person	Suele	Suelen

As you can see, it's a radical changing verb. But note that, when we use *soler* with a reflexive verb, the reflexive pronoun is added on to the infinitive like this:-

Suelo levantarme a las ocho = I normally get up at 8.00 o'clock.

Mi hermano suele dormirse a las nueve y media = My brother normally goes to bed at 9.30.

Los españoles suelen acostarse muy tarde los fines de semana = the Spanish normally go to bed late at the weekend.

Exercise 4.9

Lee o escucha y contesta las preguntas

Un día en la vida de un conserje de colegio

ANTONIO trabaja como conserje en la Academia Santa Teresa en Málaga. Es un colegio mixto y privado.

Suele levantarse bastante temprano: sobre las seis y media de la mañana. Primero se ducha y luego se viste. No le gusta desayunar mucho así que sólo toma un café con leche.

Su casa está a veinte minutos del colegio en coche. Suele llegar a las ocho menos cuarto – ¡llega siempre el primero! Abre el colegio: es decir, la cancela, las clases, el laboratorio, la biblioteca, la sala de profesores y la capilla.

Sobre las diez suele tomar un bocadillo y un café. Durante el día es responsable del mantenimiento del colegio: arregla las puertas, las pizarras, las cerraduras, las luces, los proyectores etc. y si hay algún problema intenta solucionarlo. ¡Hace muchas "chapuzas"!

Su día laboral termina a las tres de la tarde cuando va a su casa y no vuelve hasta el día siguiente. Trabaja de lunes a sábado pero los sábados empieza a las nueve, y ¡qué suerte ese día! No hay clases, no hay niños ...

Vocabulario
El conserje = caretaker
Mixto = mixed
Privado = private
Temprano = early
En coche = by car
Llegar = to arrive
Abrir = to open
Es decir = that's to say
La cancela = iron gate
La biblioteca = library
La capilla = chapel
Arreglar = to fix
La puerta = door
La cerradura = lock
La luz = light
Intentar = to try
La "chapuza" = "odd job"
Siguiente = following
¡Qué suerte! = how lucky!

1. *¿A qué hora suele levantarse Antonio?*
2. *¿Qué toma para desayunar?*
3. *¿Vive lejos del colegio?*
4. *¿Cuándo llega al colegio?*
5. *¿Qué hace cuando llega?*
6. *¿Qué come sobre las diez?*
7. *¿Cómo es su trabajo durante el día?*
8. *¿Cuándo termina su día en el colegio?*
9. *¿Cuántos días trabaja a la semana?*
10. *¿Por qué prefiere trabajar los sábados?*

Exercise 4.10

¡Escribe en español!

1. I normally get up at 7.30.
2. You normally wash before breakfast.
3. He normally listens to his CD player on the way to school.
4. We don't normally talk very much on the bus.
5. You normally go to bed at 10.00 o'clock.
6. They normally have a shower very early on Mondays.

Vocabulario

El compact disc = the CD player
De camino = on the way

Exercise 4.11

¡Lee y empareja 1-6 *con* a-l!

You receive the following letter from your Spanish friend, Roberto:

¡Hola amigo¡ ¿ Qué tal? Te escribo sobre mi familia y mi rutina diaria. Bueno, somos 4 en mi familia: mi padre, mi madre, mi hermana y yo. Mi padre tiene 36 años y es médico. Trabaja en un hospital en el centro de Granada. Mi madre, que es argentina, es su secretaria. Los dos trabajan juntos en el mismo hospital. Mi hermana mayor estudia en la universidad de Granada pero todavía vive en nuestra casa.
Es muy simpática y me llevo bien con ella. Yo tengo 14 años y estudio en el colegio San Diego aquí en Granada. Soy delgado pero muy deportista. Suelo despertarme muy temprano porque practico la natación antes de desayunar. Me levanto normalmente a las cinco y cuarto. Después de desayunar me ducho y me visto. Regreso a las seis y media, cenamos a las nueve y suelo acostarme a las once menos cuarto.

Saludos de Roberto

Vocabulario

El médico = the doctor

Juntos = together
Mismo = same
Todavía = still
Llevarse bien con = to get on well with

Desportista = sporty

La natación = swimming
Antes de (+ infin.) = before
Después de (+ infin.) = after
Regresar = to return

1.	*Hay cuatro personas*	a)	*trabajan juntos*
2.	*Sus padres*	b)	*en Granada*
3.	*Su madre*	c)	*estudian en Granada*
4.	*Roberto y su hermana*	d)	*se ducha antes de desayunar*
5.	*Roberto*	e)	*en su familia*
6.	*Se acuesta*	f)	*son médicos*
		g)	*vive en Argentina*
		h)	*se duchan*
		i)	*se ducha después de nadar*
		j)	*a las 11.45*
		k)	*a las 10.45*
		l)	*es de Argentina*

Exercise 4.12

¡Escucha!
Indica si las frases son verdaderas (V) or falsas (F)

1.   *Alfonso se despierta a las siete y media.*
2.   *Alfonso se ducha después de despertarse.*
3.   *Laura se viste antes de desayunar.*
4.   *Miguel siempre se levanta a las siete.*
5.   *Victoria se ducha antes de desayunar.*
6.   *Los fines de semana, Luis se acuesta muy tarde.*

> **Vocabulario**
> *En seguida* = right away
> *De la madruga* = in the early morning
> *La madrugada* = the dawn.

Exercise 4.13

¡Habla!
In pairs, ask and answer the following questions. Answer as fully as you can, using the verb *soler* where appropriate.

1.   *¿A qué hora te despiertas por la mañana?*
2.   *¿A qué hora te levantas?*
3.   *¿Dónde te lavas?*
4.   *¿Te duchas?*
5.   *¿Dónde te vistes?*
6.   *¿Dónde desayunas?*
7.   *¿A qué hora te acuestas durante la semana?*
8.   *¿A qué hora te acuestas los fines de semana?*

Exercise 4.14

La rutina diaria de Miguel
1.   *¡Lee!*

Miguel <u>suele</u> *despertarse a las siete y media.* <u>Se levanta</u> *diez minutos después.* <u>Se lava</u>, <u>se viste</u> *y luego* <u>desayuna</u>: *normalmente un café con leche y tostadas.* <u>Estudia</u> *en el colegio de 9 a 2. Luego* <u>come</u> *en casa. Por la tarde* <u>ve</u> *la televisión y* <u>cena</u> *y* <u>se acuesta</u> *a las diez.*

2.   *¡Escribe!*

Rewrite the passage to give your own daily routine, making any changes that you think necessary. In particular, be sure to change the underlined verbs to the first person singular of that verb.

Exercise 4.15

¡Escribe!
Mi hermana, Bea.
Mira y escribe en español la rutina diaria de Bea Hernandez:

¡Vocabulario!

Keep working away at the vocabulary. The more you learn by heart, the easier things become.

Vocabulario 4.1

Abrir	= to open	*El coche*	= car
Acostarse (ue)	= to go to bed	*La biblioteca*	= library
Almorzar (ue)	= to have lunch	*La capilla*	= chapel
Bañarse	= to have a bath, to bathe	*La luz*	= light
Despertarse (ie)	= to wake up	*La rutina*	= routine
Dormir (ue)	= to sleep	*La sala de profesores*	= staff room
Ducharse	= to have a shower		
Intentar	= to try	*Privado*	= private
Lavarse	= to have a wash	*Sólo*	= only
Levantarse	= to get up	*Tarde*	= late
Limpiarse los dientes	= to brush one's teeth	*Temprano*	= early
Llegar	= to arrive		
Peinarse	= to comb one's hair	*Entonces*	= then
Quitarse la ropa	= to get undressed	*Luego*	= then
Regresar	= to return	*Si*	= if
Volver (ue)	= to go back/return	*Todavía*	= still
		Un poco	= a little

Antes de (+ infin.)	= before doing …
Después de (+ infin.)	= after doing …

Estar

We are already familiar with the verb *ser* = to be, which we use to tell us **who** or **what** something is. If however we wish to say **where** something is, we use another verb, *estar*.

Here's the verb in full:

	Singular	Plural
1st person	*estoy*	*estamos*
2nd person	*estás*	*estáis*
3rd person	*está*	*están*

E.g. *¿Dónde está Juan?*
Juan está en el jardín.

E.g. *¿Dónde estás?*
Estoy en el jardín.

Prepositions

Now that we know how to say where something is, using *estar*, we can learn about prepositions.
A preposition is used before a noun, generally to tell us something about the **position** of that noun.

E.g.   The father is **next to** the mother.
E.g.   The brother is **behind** the sister.

Vocabulario

Al lado de	= next to	*Detrás de*	= behind
Cerca de	= near to	*En*	= in, on
Con	= with	*Enfrente de*	= opposite
Debajo de	= under	*Lejos de*	= far from
Delante de	= in front of	*Sobre*	= above/on top of/on

As most of these end in the word *de*, don't forget to observe the golden rule which we met when we learnt about possession:

De + el = ***del***
E.g. *al lado [**de el**] padre = al lado **del** padre.*

Exercise 4.16

¡Mira y escribe!
¿Dónde están?

1.   *¿Dónde está el padre?*
2.   *¿Dónde están los niños?*
3.   *¿Dónde está la madre?*
4.   *¿Dónde está la abuela?*
5.   *¿Dónde está el abuelo?*

Exercise 4.17

¡Lee y escucha!

Me llamo Joaquín. Vivo en un piso; está en el centro de Barcelona. Es un piso grande y cómodo.

Yo me llamo Charo. Vivo en un chalet moderno; está en la sierra, cerca de Madrid.

Me llamo Josefina. Vivo en una casa en el campo en las afueras de Santiago de Compostela.

Me llamo Basilio. Vivo en Colombia en una chabola.

Me llamo Alfredo. Vivo en una granja pequeña en Costa Rica.

¡Contesta las preguntas!

¿Dónde viven?

1. *¿Dónde vive Joaquín?*
2. *¿Cómo es su piso?*
3. *¿Quién vive en un chalet?*
4. *¿Dónde está el chalet?*
5. *¿Cómo es?*
6. *¿Dónde vive Josefina?*
7. *¿Vive en la ciudad?*
8. *¿Quién vive en Colombia?*
9. *¿Vive Basilio en un piso?*
10. *¿Vive Alfredo en una chabola?*
11. *¿Dónde está su granja?*
12. *¿Cómo es?*

> **Vocabulario**
> *La casa* = the house
> *La granja* = the farm
> *La chabola* = the shack
> *El piso* = the flat
> *El chalet* = the detached house
> *El centro* = the centre
> *El campo* = the countryside
> *La sierra* = the mountains
> *La ciudad* = the city
> *Las afueras* = the outskirts

Exercise 4.18

¡Habla y escribe!
¿Dónde vives? ¿Cómo es?

¿Ser o estar?

Now that you know both verbs 'to be', be sure that you know when to use each one:

1. **Ser** is used to say:
    - **Who** someone is
    - **What** something is
    - **What nationality** someone is
    - **What** someone or something is like (permanently)

    E.g. *¿Quién **es**? **Es** mi padre.*
    *¿Qué **es**? **Es** una mesa.*
    *¿De qué nacionalidad **es**? **Es** alemán.*
    *¿Cómo **es** tu casa? **Es** grande.*

2. **Estar** is used to say:
    - **Where** someone or something is
    - **What** someone or something is like (temporarily)

    E.g. *¿Dónde **está** tu madre? **Está** en la cocina.*
    *¿Cómo **estás**? **Estoy** muy bien.*

Exercise 4.19

Traduce al español con SER

1. Who's that? It's my teacher – he's French.
2. Who are they? They're my parents.
3. What are they like? They're very kind.
4. Who are you? I'm Paquita and I'm Spanish.
5. Who are you? I'm Alfredo and I'm Argentinian.
6. What's your grandmother like?
7. What nationality are you?
8. We are German.
9. You are a teacher, aren't you?
10. What are your pupils like?
11. What's this?
12. What are you like?

Exercise 4.20

Traduce al español con ESTAR

1. Where is Madrid? It's in the centre of Spain.
2. Where are the children? They're at school.
3. Where are you? (familiar, singular) I'm at home.
4. Where are you? (polite, singular) I'm in the classroom.
5. Where are you, Luis and Juan? (familiar, plural)
6. We're in the market square.
7. Where is your house?
8. It's near the station.
9. Where's your sister?
10. She's at university.
11. How are you today? I am okay, thanks.
12. How is your father today? He is very well.

Exercise 4.21

¡Escribe!

*Completa las frases con la persona adecuada del verbo **ser** o **estar**.*

1. Mi padre ___ galés.
2. Mi casa ___ en Londres.
3. ¿Cómo ___ tus hermanos?
4. Mis abuelos ___ en el jardín.
5. Nosotros ___ en el colegio.
6. Tú ___ español; ¿verdad?
7. Yo ___ alumna.
8. Usted ___ profesor.
9. ¿Dónde ___ usted?
10. Mamá, yo ___ en el cuarto de baño.
11. Tus amigos ___ muy simpáticos.
12. Vosotros ___ muy pesados hoy.

Exercise 4.22

¡Habla!

Pregunta a tu compañero/a. Contesta en frases completas.

1. ¿Dónde está tu casa?
2. ¿Dónde está tu instituto?
3. ¿Dónde está tu libro de español?
4. ¿Dónde está tu profesor?
5. ¿Dónde están tus padres?
6. ¿Qué es? (pick up an object)
7. ¿Cómo es tu mejor amigo?
8. ¿Qué hora es?
9. ¿Cómo es tu profesor de español?
10. ¿Cómo es tu casa?

Exercise 4.23

¡Escribe en inglés!

1. Mi madre está en el cuarto de baño.
2. Mis animales están en el jardín.
3. Estamos en el colegio.
4. Los tíos están en Sevilla.
5. Los chicos están en su dormitorio.

Exercise 4.24

¡Escribe en español!

1. The girl is in her bedroom.
2. The boys are in the garden.
3. My father is in the bathroom.
4. My grandparents are in the kitchen.
5. His dog is in the hall.

Exercise 4.25

¡Lee o escucha!

SANTA BARBARA

Santa Bárbara es patrona de las armas de artillería y de los trabajadores de minas y explosivos. El día de Santa Bárbara se celebra el 2 de diciembre.

Según una vieja tradición, Santa Bárbara era hija de un hombre muy rudo llamado Dióscoro.

Ella no cree en los ídolos paganos de su padre, por lo que él la encierra en un castillo con dos ventanas pero ella manda añadir una tercera ventana para acordarse de las Tres Divinas Personas de la Santísima Trinidad. Por esto su padre se pone furioso y permite que la martiricen: le cortan la cabeza con una espada.

Así, Santa Bárbara es representada con una espada y una corona porque es una mártir. La misma tradición dice que a su padre le cae un rayo y lo mata. Por este motivo, muchas personas rezan a la Santa para pedir protección contra los rayos de las tormentas.

Vocabulario	
La patrona	= patron
Era	= (she) was
Rudo	= rough
Llamado	= called
Creer	= to believe
Encerrar (ie)	= to shut up
El Castillo	= castle
Mandar	= to order
Añadir	= to add
Acordarse (ue)	= to remember
Ponerse furioso	= to get angry
Martirizar	= to torture
Cortar	= to cut
La cabeza	= the head
La espada	= the sword
La corona	= the crown
Hacerse	= to become
Mismo	= same
Caer	= to fall
El rayo	= the lightning
Matar	= to kill
Rezar	= to pray
Pedir (i)	= to ask for
La tormenta	= the storm

Contesta las preguntas:

1. *¿Santa Bárbara es santa de qué?*
2. *¿Cuándo es el día de Santa Bárbara?*
3. *¿Cómo se llama el padre de Santa Bárbara?*
4. *¿Cómo es?*
5. *¿Por qué su padre la encierra en un castillo?*
6. *¿Cuántas ventanas tiene el castillo?*
7. *¿Cómo la matan?*
8. *¿Qué mata a su padre?*

Los números 100-1000

100	*Cien*
110	*Ciento diez*
200	*Doscientos*
300	*Trescientos*
400	*Cuatrocientos*
500	*Quinientos*
600	*Seiscientos*
700	*Setecientos*
800	*Ochocientos*
900	*Novecientos*
1,000	*Mil*

N.B. When we use these numbers on their own they are always masculine. If however we are using them with a feminine noun, the **–os** becomes **–as**.

E.g. *Doscien**tos** euros*
*Doscien**tas** chicas*

Note also that *ciento* (=100) is always shortened to *cien*.

E.g. *¿Cuántos euros hay en la mesa? Hay **cien** euros en la mesa.*

Ordinals

1st	*Primero/a*
2nd	*Segundo/a*
3rd	*Tercero/a*
4th	*Cuarto/a*
5th	*Quinto/a*
6th	*Sexto/a*
7th	*Séptimo/a*
8th	*Octavo/a*
9th	*Noveno/a*
10th	*Décimo/a*

¿Cuántos euros hay?

Note

1. Remember that the ordinals are adjectives, and must agree with the nouns they go with.
E.g. *Tome **la primera calle** a la derecha* = Take the 1st street on the right.

2. The ordinals *primero* and *tercero* must be apocopated (scary long word for "cut short") in front of a masculine noun.
E.g. *¿Dónde vives?* *Vivo en el **primer[o]** piso.*
    ¿Y tú? *Yo vivo en la **tercera** planta.*

3. Remember that the ordinals are **not** used to give dates.
E.g. *El **uno** de mayo; el **dos** de mayo; el **tres** de mayo; etc.*

¿Cuál es tu dirección?

Finding your way around in a foreign country can be made even more stressful if you don't understand the format for addresses. So here are some basics, with a few examples:

1. After the person's name, we get the street they live in, often abbreviated to c/ for *calle*.
2. Then we get the building or house number.
3. Then we get the floor.
4. Then we get the flat or appartment, which will be a letter (e.g. A to F).
5. Then we get the post code and town.

So, Sr. Domínguez, below, lives in a street called José Clara, in building 22, and in flat A. It is probably quite a small building as the floors are not numbered.

```
Sr. Rafael Beloso Domínguez
c/ José Clara 22-A
VILAFORTUNY 43858
(Tarragona)
ESPAÑA
```

```
Sra. Pilar Palacín Melero
Vía Roma 5-5°A
43840 SALOU
```

```
Sr. Santiago del Amo Rodríguez
c/ Martínez Maldonado 14-4°B
29007 MÁLAGA
```

```
Sra. Lily Blanco
Apdo. Postal 916
2150 MORAVIA
(San José)
COSTA RICA
```

```
Srta. Raquel Haro Gutiérrez
c/ Cáceres 34-7°D
28922 Alcorcón
MADRID
```

Vocabulario	
Señor (Sr.)	= Mr.
Señora (Sra.)	= Mrs.
Señorita (Srta.)	= Miss
La calle (C/)	= street
La carretera	= road
El apartado postal (Apdo. Postal)	= PO Box
El piso (°)	= floor
La planta	= floor

Exercise 4.26

¡Lee y escribe en inglés!

Look at the addresses given above and write out in English a full description of who each letter is addressed to and precisely where each person lives.

Exercise 4.27

¡Escucha!

Completa la agenda de direcciones.

1. Leticia
2. Ignacio
3. Helena
4. Luis
5. Francisco
6. Ann

La casa

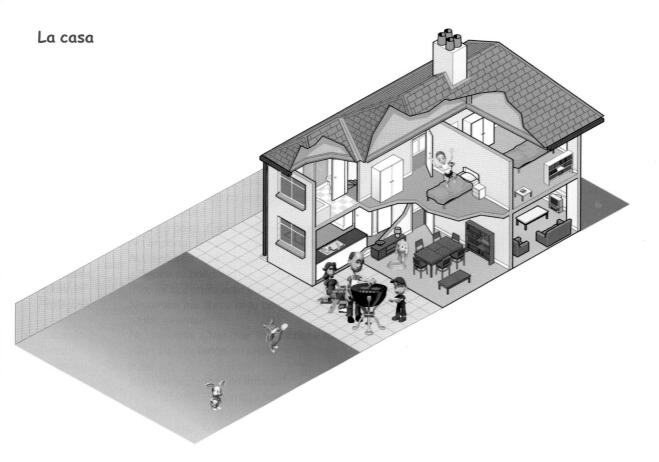

Exercise 4.28

¡Habla!

¿Dónde están? Mira el dibujo.

Ejemplo:

"¿Dónde está el conejo?" "El conejo está en el jardín."

1.   El padre
2.   La madre
3.   El chico
4.   La chica
5.   El perro
6.   El gato

Exercise 4.29

¡Escucha!

¿Dónde están?:

1.   *Los padres de Maribel están en ....*
2.   *Su hermano, que se llama Francisco está en...............*
3.   *Su abuelo está sentado en...............*
4.   *Maribel está en ....*

> **Vocabulario**
> El árbol = tree
> El comedor = dining room
> El cuarto de baño = bathroom
> El dormitorio = bedroom
> El jardín = garden
> El salón = living room
> El techo = ceiling
> El tejado = roof
> El vestíbulo = hall
> El wáter = lavatory
> La cocina = kitchen
> La terraza = terrace

Los muebles

We are now going to learn what furniture we find in which room, beginning with the sitting room.

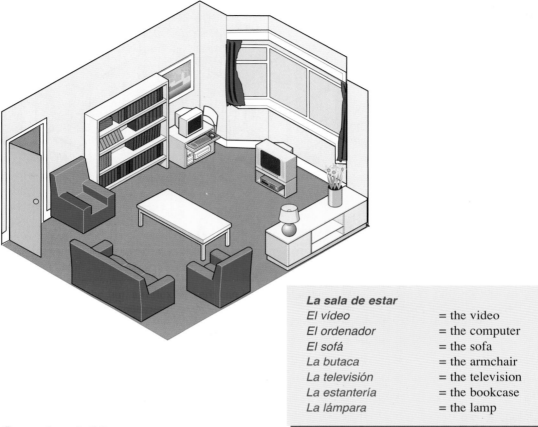

La sala de estar	
El vídeo	= the video
El ordenador	= the computer
El sofá	= the sofa
La butaca	= the armchair
La televisión	= the television
La estantería	= the bookcase
La lámpara	= the lamp

Exercise 4.30

¡Mira y escribe!

1. *¿Dónde están las butacas?*
2. *¿Dónde está el sofá?*
3. *¿Dónde está la lámpara?*

4. *¿Dónde está la televisión?*
5. *¿Dónde está el vídeo?*
6. *¿Dónde está el ordenador?*

Exercise 4.31

¡Habla!
Escucha, lee y luego practica la conversación con tu pareja, e inventa un diálogo parecido.

En casa de los Trujillo

Madre:	*Oye, Paco, ¿dónde estás?*
Paco:	*Estoy aquí, mamá, en el sofá en la sala de estar.*
Madre:	*¿Qué haces?*
Paco:	*Hay un buen programa en la tele así que...*
Madre:	*Pero tienes muchos deberes, ¿no?*
Paco:	*Sí, mamá pero prefiero ver mi programa favorito o jugar con el ordenador...*
Madre:	*Pero ¡Qué pesado eres, hijo!*

Exercise 4.32

¡Lee y habla!

En el dormitorio de Paco

Es una habitación bastante grande con las paredes pintadas de azul claro. Hay muchos pósters. Cerca de la ventana hay una cama y al lado una mesita de noche con una lámpara muy moderna. A mano izquierda, delante de la puerta, hay un armario y una estantería con muchos libros. En el suelo hay una alfombra pequeña de muchos colores.

1. *Lee el párrafo y traduce al inglés.*
2. *Mira el dibujo y luego tapa la descripción.*
3. *Ahora describe el dormitorio a tu pareja. Tu pareja puede ayudarte con preguntas.*

Ejemplo

¿Dónde está la cama?
¿Qué hay en las paredes?
¿Qué hay en la mesita de noche?
¿Qué hay en el suelo?
¿Qué hay a la izquierda?

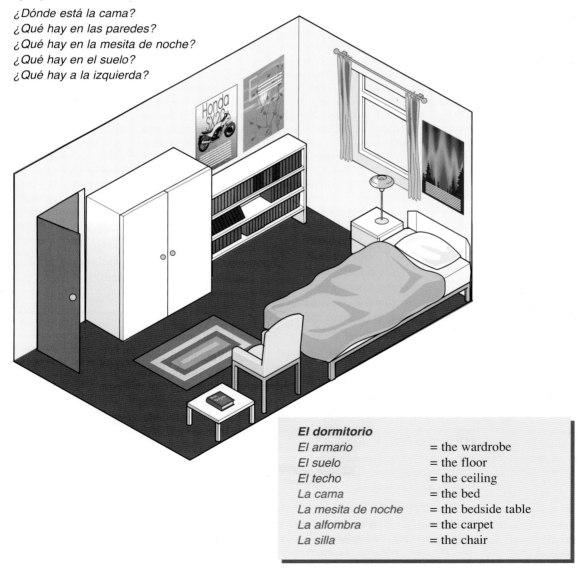

El dormitorio	
El armario	= the wardrobe
El suelo	= the floor
El techo	= the ceiling
La cama	= the bed
La mesita de noche	= the bedside table
La alfombra	= the carpet
La silla	= the chair

La cocina

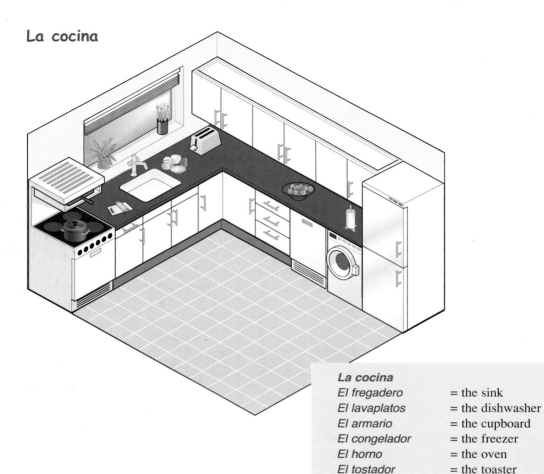

La cocina	
El fregadero	= the sink
El lavaplatos	= the dishwasher
El armario	= the cupboard
El congelador	= the freezer
El horno	= the oven
El tostador	= the toaster
La nevera	= the fridge
La lavadora	= the washing-machine
La parrilla	= the grill

Exercise 4.33

¡Lee y escucha!
En la cocina

A las 9, la señora Trujillo **lava** *los platos del desayuno en el fregadero.*

A las 10 **pone** *la lavadora y después tiende la ropa.*

Cinco minutos después **friega** *el suelo.*

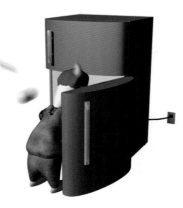

*Sobre las 12.30 **empieza** a preparar la comida. Saca el pescado y las verduras de la nevera.*

*Media hora después **mete** el pescado en el horno y **cuece** las verduras.*

*A las 2 en punto **lleva** la comida a la mesa del comedor.*

*Después de comer **prepara** un café para su marido.*

*Sobre las 3.30 **pone** los platos sucios en el lavaplatos.*

¡Escribe!

Contesta las preguntas

1. *¿Qué hace la señora Trujillo a las 10?*
2. *¿A qué hora empieza a preparar la comida?*
3. *¿Cuándo friega el suelo?*
4. *¿De dónde saca el pescado?*
5. *¿La familia Trujillo come en la cocina?*
6. *¿Para quién prepara un café?*
7. *¿Dónde pone los platos sucios?*
8. *¿Y a qué hora?*

> **Vocabulario**
> | | |
> |---|---|
> | Poner | = to put (on) |
> | Tender (ie) | = to hang out |
> | Meter | = to put |
> | Sacar | = to take out |
> | Llevar | = to take/carry |
> | Cocer (ue) | = to cook |
> | Sobre | = about (of time) |
> | En punto | = on the dot |
> | Sucio | = dirty |
> | Para | = for |

El comedor

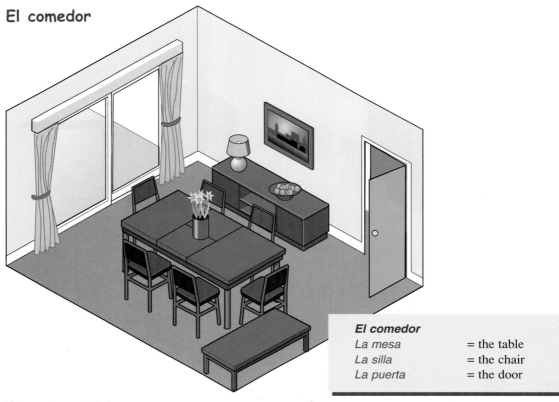

El comedor

La mesa	= the table
La silla	= the chair
La puerta	= the door

Exercise 4.34

¡Escucha!

En el comedor

1. *¿Qué hora es?*
2. *¿Qué hay de primer plato?*
3. *¿Está contento Paco (el chico)?*
4. *¿Por qué?*
5. *¿Cómo está la sopa?*

6. *¿Qué tal el colegio?*
7. *¿Qué comen de segundo plato?*
8. *¿Qué hay de postre?*
9. *¿A qué hora vuelve a la oficina el padre?*
10. *¿A Paco, ¿qué comida le gusta mucho?*

Vocabulario

Sopa de fideos	= noodle soup
Ya	= already
¡Venga!	= come on!
¡Anda!	= come on!
Riquísimo	= delicious
Callarse	= to be quiet
O sea	= that is, i.e
Lubina a la sal	= sea bass cooked in salt
Para chuparse los dedos	= delicious (lit. to suck one's fingers)
Flan con nata	= crème caramel with cream

EN EL CUARTO DE BAÑO

07:00

07:10

07:20

07:30

Exercise 4.35

¡Escribe!
Mira los dibujos y escribe lo que hace Paco.
Tienes que utilizar <u>un verbo reflexivo</u> para cada frase.
¿Qué hace Paco?

1. ....
2. ....
3. ....
4. ....

El cuarto de baño

El lavabo	= the basin
El wáter*	= the lavatory
El espejo	= the mirror
La ducha	= the shower
La bañera	= the bath

*This word is pronounced with a V sound.
The word *wáter* has been adopted into
Spanish from English and is spelled with
the letter *w*, a letter that is not really used
in the Spanish alphabet!

Word order

You have probably noticed, but we are going to tell you anyway, that in Spanish, the subject is often placed **after** its verb, both in statements and in questions.

E.g. *¿Qué hace Paco?*
Escribe lo que hace Paco.

Try to imitate this practice in your spoken and written Spanish; it's bound to impress!

Exercise 4.36

¡Dibuja y escribe!
1. *Dibuja un plano de tu casa.*
2. *¿Cómo es tu casa?*
3. *Describe dónde están los muebles.*

Exercise 4.37

¡Habla!
Pregunta a tu pareja sobre:
1. *las actividades en cada habitación;*
2. *los muebles de cada habitación.*

Ejemplo 1.

¿Qué haces en:
● *la sala de estar?*
● *la cocina?*
● *tu dormitorio?*
● *el comedor?*
● *el cuarto de baño?*

¿A qué hora:
● *te levantas?*
● *te acuestas?*

¿Dónde:
● *ves la televisión?*
● *te lavas?*
● *desayunas?*
● *comes?*
● *escuchas música?*
● *haces los deberes?*
● *duermes?*

Ejemplo 2.

¿Qué muebles hay en:
● *la sala de estar?*
● *el comedor?*
● *la cocina?*

¿Dónde está:
● *el dormitorio de tus padres?*
● *tu dormitorio?*
● *el cuarto de baño?*
● *la televisión?*
● *el sofá?*
● *el teléfono?*

Decir (i) = to say, tell

Here's another useful little verb to bring joy into your troubled lives. Note the silly *g* in the first person singular.

	Singular	**Plural**
1st person	*Digo*	*Decimos*
2nd person	*Dices*	*Decís*
3rd person	*Dice*	*Dicen*

Vocabulario 4.2

El comedor	= the dining room	*El campo*	= the countryside
El cuarto de baño	= the bathroom	*El centro*	= the centre
El dormitorio	= the bedroom	*La carretera*	= the road
La cocina	= the kitchen	*La calle*	= the street
La sala de estar	= the sitting-room	*La granja*	= the farm
		La sierra	= the mountains
El armario	= the wardrobe, cupboard	*La vía*	= way
El congelador	= the freezer		
El espejo	= the mirror	*Acordarse (ue)*	= to remember
El fregadero	= the sink	*Añadir*	= to add
El horno	= the oven	*Caer*	= to fall
El lavabo	= the basin	*Celebrar*	= to celebrate
El lavaplatos	= the dishwasher	*Cocer (ue)*	= to cook
El sofá	= the sofa	*Cortar*	= to cut
El suelo	= the floor	*Decir (i)*	= to say
El techo	= the ceiling	*Hacerse*	= to become
El tostador	= the toaster	*Llevar*	= to take/carry
El vídeo	= the video	*Mandar*	= to give orders
El wáter	= the lavatory	*Meter*	= to put
		Permitir	= to allow
La alfombra	= the carpet	*Poner*	= to put (on)
La bañera	= the bath	*Rezar*	= to pray
La butaca	= the armchair	*Sacar*	= to take out
La cama	= the bed		
La ducha	= the shower	*Al lado de*	= next to
La estantería	= the bookcase	*Cerca de*	= near to
La lámpara	= the lamp	*Delante de*	= in front of
La lavadora	= the washing-machine	*Detrás de*	= behind
La mesita de noche	= the bedside table	*Enfrente de*	= opposite
La nevera	= the fridge	*Lejos de*	= far from
La parrilla	= the grill	*Para*	= for
La puerta	= the door		
La televisión	= the television		

Deberes

¡Investiga!

Work in pairs or individually to produce a display or presentation illustrating the life-style and daily routine of someone living in a Spanish–speaking country. Produce a commentary in Spanish to accompany your work.

Expectations

At the end of this unit

You should be able to: understand and use reflexive verbs to describe and ask questions about daily routines; talk and write about your home and what you do at home; understand and use numbers greater than 100 and give an address in Spanish; describe a room, orally and in writing, saying where items of furniture are.

You may also be able to: understand a more detailed written or spoken text about where people live; memorise and use vocabulary and all persons of verbs; use a glossary or dictionary effectively.

About the unit

In this unit you will learn about places in town and how to ask for and give simple directions. You will learn to talk about the weather and the names of countries.

New contexts:

- places in town
- points of the compass and maps
- following and giving directions
- seasons
- weather

New language content:

- the irregular verb *ir*
- positive imperative form of regular verbs

El pueblo

We are now going to learn how to find our way around the town.

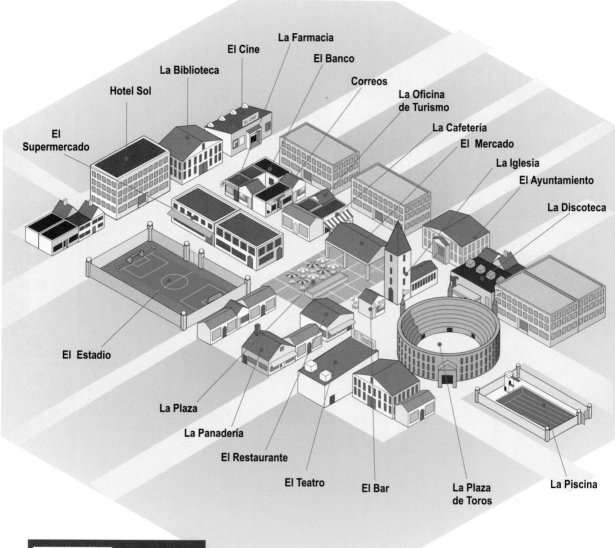

La Farmacia
El Cine
La Biblioteca
El Banco
Hotel Sol
Correos
La Oficina de Turismo
El Supermercado
La Cafetería
El Mercado
La Iglesia
El Ayuntamiento
La Discoteca
El Estadio
La Plaza
La Panadería
El Restaurante
El Teatro
El Bar
La Plaza de Toros
La Piscina

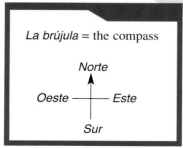

La brújula = the compass

Norte
Oeste — Este
Sur

Vocabulario

El ayuntamiento	= the town hall	*La biblioteca*	= the library
El banco	= the bank	*La cafetería*	= the café
El bar	= the bar	*La catedral*	= the cathedral
El cine	= the cinema	*La discoteca*	= the discotheque
El estadio	= the sports stadium	*La estación*	= the station
El hotel	= the hotel	*La farmacia*	= the chemist
El mercado	= the market	*La iglesia*	= the church
El pueblo	= the town	*La panadería*	= the bakery
El restaurante	= the restaurant	*La piscina*	= the swimming pool
El supermercado	= the supermarket	*La plaza*	= the square
El teatro	= the theatre	*La plaza de toros*	= the bullring
Correos	= the post office	*La tienda*	= the shop

Exercise 5.1

¡Escucha!
¿Dónde está?
Estás de vacaciones en España y decides visitar la Oficina de Turismo. Escuchas varias conversaciones. Escucha estas conversaciones con cuidado y luego escribe dónde están los siguientes sitios:

1. *La farmacia*
2. *El teatro y la plaza de toros*
3. *La iglesia*
4. *El supermercado*

Exercise 5.2

¡Escribe en español!

1. The theatre is quite far from here. It's near the bullring.
2. The discotheque is behind the church.
3. The bakery is opposite the market.
4. The cathedral is on the outskirts of the town.
5. The bullring is near the bar.
6. The church is opposite the town hall.
7. The stadium is near to the supermarket.
8. The chemist is very near the post office.

> **N.B.** The masculine noun *correo* (= post) is used (without an article) in the plural for Post Office.
> E.g. *Voy a Correos* = I am going to the post office.
> *¿Donde está Correos?* = Where is the post office?

Exercise 5.3

¡Habla!
Mira el mapa. ¿Dónde está?
Study the map on page 110. Take it in turns with your partner to explain where the following places are:

1. *La plaza*
2. *El mercado*
3. *El hotel*
4. *El teatro*
5. *La panadería*
6. *La piscina*
7. *La plaza de toros*
8. *El banco*

En España

As you may well know, a bullring is round yet it's called *la plaza* (the square).
This is because the first official bullfights took place in the Town Square.

Ir = to go

Now we need to learn this very important irregular verb:

	Singular	**Plural**
1st person	*Voy*	*Vamos*
2nd person	*Vas*	*Vais*
3rd person	*Va*	*Van*

This verb is always followed by the preposition *a* = to, but remember : *a + el = al.*

E.g.   *Voy a + el restaurante = Voy **al** restaurante.*
       *Voy a + el mercado = Voy **al** mercado.*

¿Adónde vas?

Hoy yo voy al bar.

Los sábados vamos a la discoteca.

Tú vas al teatro, ¿verdad?

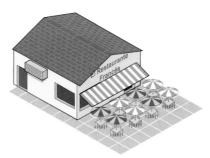

Vosotros vais al restaurante francés.

Mi madre va a la farmacia a comprar aspirinas.

Los domingos mis padres van a la iglesia.

Exercise 5.4

¡Habla y escribe!
¿Cómo se dice en español?

1. I'm going to the bullring.
2. You're going to the station. (Familiar singular)
3. My family goes to church on Sundays.
4. We do not go to school on Saturdays.
5. Do you go to the cinema in the evenings? (Polite singular)
6. Are you going to the town? (Familiar plural)
7. My sisters always go to the shops.
8. You go to the supermarket. (Polite plural)

Exercise 5.5

¡Escucha!
Rellena la ficha
Say where each person is going and where exactly the place is.

	¿Adónde va?	¿Dónde está exactamente?
Alfredo	....	....
Isabel	....	....
Rafael	....	....
Mari-Carmen	....	....
Raquel	....	....

¿Por dónde se va a?

We now need to know how to arrive at a place.

1. To say 'how do I get to?' we say:
   ¿Por dónde se va a?
   Eg   *¿Por dónde se va a la farmacia?* = how do I get to the Chemist's?
        ¿Por dónde se va a la catedral? = how do I get to the cathedral?
        ¿Por dónde se va al ayuntamiento? = How do I get to the town-hall?

2. In answer to the question: *¿Por dónde se va a ......?* we can use:
   Hay que + Infinitive; or
   Tiene que + Infinitive.
   E.g. *Hay que subir / Tiene que subir esta calle.*
         You have to go up this street.
   E.g. *Hay que tomar / Tiene que tomar la primera calle a la derecha.*
         You have to take the first street on the right.

You will normally be using the polite form in this sort of situation, but obviously if you were talking to someone you knew well *tiene que* would become *tienes que*.

Vocabulario

Bajar = to go down
Cruzar = to cross
Doblar = to turn
Tomar = to take

Coger = to take
Subir = to go up
Seguir (i) = to continue/carry on

Exercise 5.6

¡Escribe en inglés!

1. "*¿Por dónde se va a la panadería?*"
   "*Tiene que seguir todo recto y tomar la segunda a la izquierda.*"

2. "*¿Por dónde se va al Banco de España?*"
   "*Hay que doblar a la derecha, y el banco está enfrente del supermercado Aurrerá.*"

3. "*¿Por dónde se va al Teatro Cervantes?*"
   "*Tiene que bajar esta calle, y luego coger la primera a la izquierda. Está a cien metros.*"

4. "*¿Por dónde se va al Mercado Municipal?*"
   "*Hay que seguir hasta la estación. Está enfrente.*"

Exercise 5.7

¡Habla!

In pairs, using the map below, practise asking how to arrive at various places and giving the directions.

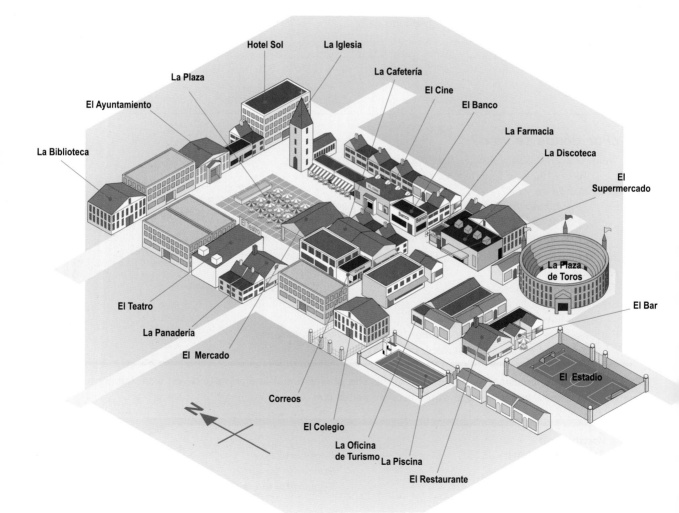

Imperatives: polite form

Another way of giving directions is to use the imperative. When speaking to a stranger in the street we use the polite singular form if addressing one person, the polite plural form if we are addressing more than one person.

AR Verbs	Singular	Plural	
Tomar	tom-e	tom-en	take!
Bajar	baj-e	baj-en	go down!
Cruzar	cruc-e*	cruc-en	cross!
Doblar	dobl-e	dobl-en	turn!

* **N.B.** The z changes to c.

ER Verbs			
Coger	*coj-a	coj-an	take!

***N.B.** The g changes to j in the imperative in order to keep the same pronunciation as in the infinitive.

IR Verbs			
Subir	sub-a	sub-an	go up!
Seguir (i)	sig-a	sig-an	continue!

Note			
AR verbs:	E	EN	
ER and IR verbs:	A	AN	

Irregular

The verb ir is irregular and has the following imperatives:

Ir	vaya	vayan	go!

Exercise 5.8

Escucha y para cada una de las 5 personas contesta las preguntas:

a)   ¿Adónde quieren ir?

b)   ¿Cómo tienen que ir?

Exercise 5.9

¡Lee y escribe en inglés!

1.   ¿Por dónde se va al castillo, por favor?
     Tome la primera calle a la izquierda.

2.   ¿Por dónde se va a la plaza mayor,
     por favor?
     Tome la segunda calle a la derecha.

3.   ¿Por dónde se va a la estación de RENFE,
     por favor?
     Tome la tercera calle a la izquierda.

4.   ¿Por dónde se va a la oficina de turismo,
     por favor?
     Cruce la plaza y está a la izquierda.

En España
RENFE is the Spanish national railway system.

Exercise 5.10

¡Traduce al español!

1. Go down the street.
2. Cross the square.
3. Continue straight ahead.
4. Take the first street on the right.
5. Take the second street on the left.
6. Turn to the right at the traffic lights.
7. Go up this street.
8. It's there, next to the church.

Vocabulario
En el semáforo = at the traffic lights
Todo recto = straight ahead
Allí = there (near)
Allá = there (far)

Exercise 5.11

¡Habla!
Mira el mapa en la pagina 114 y con tu pareja inventa un diálogo para practicar estos imperativos.

Ejemplo: *¿Por dónde se va a la discoteca?*
             Tome la primera a la derecha.

Exercise 5.12

Lee o escucha y contesta las preguntas: ¿verdad o mentira?

El Peatón:	"Perdone, señor, ¿para ir a la catedral, por favor?"
Señor:	"Lo siento, no soy de aquí."
El Peatón:	"Oiga, señorita. ¿Por dónde se va a la catedral, por favor?"
Señorita:	"¿Va Usted en coche o andando?"
El peatón:	"Andando."
Señorita:	"¡Uf, está un poco lejos!"
El peatón:	"Hable un poco más despacio, por favor. Soy extranjero."
Señorita:	"Ay, lo siento….. Pues tiene que seguir todo recto, ¿comprende?, hasta el final de esta calle. Usted verá la biblioteca municipal en la esquina. Pues, coja la calle a la derecha, que se llama Calle Princesa, y baje esa calle hasta el primer semáforo. Allí hay que cruzar la plaza y la catedral está justo enfrente. ¿Vale?"
El peatón:	"Un momento,…. todo recto hasta el final, luego a la derecha hasta el semáforo y allí tengo que cruzar la plaza, ¿no?"
Señorita :	"Eso es, señor."
El Peatón:	"Muchas gracias, señorita."

Vocabulario

El peatón = the pedestrian

Oiga = Excuse me

Andando = on foot

Despacio = slow
El extranjero = the foreigner

Usted verá = you will see
La esquina = the corner
Ese, esa = that
El semáforo = traffic-light
¿Vale? = Okay?

Eso es = That's right.

¿Verdad o mentira?
1. El peatón va a la iglesia.
2. El señor es de allí.
3. El peatón va en coche.
4. La señorita habla muy despacio.
5. La catedral está lejos.
6. El peatón tiene que cruzar la calle.
7. Hay una piscina en la esquina.
8. La calle a la derecha se llama "calle Princesa".
9. El peatón tiene que subir la calle Princesa.
10. La catedral está enfrente de la plaza.

Imperatives: familiar form

If you are giving instructions to one of your friends or somebody of your own age, you would have to use the familiar form of the imperative, rather than the polite form, and this has a different set of endings. You have been meeting these for some time, perhaps without noticing, in our instructions: *habla, escucha, lee, escribe.* Anyway, here they are now in full:

AR Verbs	Singular	Plural	
Tomar	tom-a	tom-ad	Take!
Bajar	baj-a	baj-ad	Go down!
Cruzar	cruz-a	cruz-ad	Cross
Doblar	dobl-a	dobl-ad	Turn!

ER Verbs			
Coger	cog-e	cog-ed	Take!

IR Verbs			
Subir	sub-e	sub-id	Go up!
Seguir(i)	sigu-e	segu-id	Continue/Carry on!

Note

AR verbs →	A	AD
ER verbs →	E	ED
IR verbs →	E	ID

Irregular
Again, we need to note the irregular forms of the verb *ir*:

Ir	ve	id	Go!

The plural forms of the familiar imperative are actually rarely used. Instead, the verb's infinitive is used. E.g. one would say *tomar* rather than *tomad* if one were talking to more than one friend, or to people of one's own age.

Exercise 5.13

Escucha la conversación telefónica entre 2 amigos y luego escribe las instrucciones para ir a la discoteca.
¡Vamos a la discoteca!

1. *Hay que coger el autobús número ---*
2. *...hasta el ---*
3. *Entonces hay que bajar por la---*
4. *... y cuando llegues al --- semáforo,*
5. *hay que tomar la --- a la derecha.*
6. *Entonces, hay que subir esa calle hasta ---*
7. *...y luego tomar la segunda a la ---*
8. *La discoteca está a --- metros...*
9. *...al lado de un ---.*
10. *Hay que estar allí el sábado a las ---.*

Exercise 5.14

¡Escribe!
Tienes una fiesta de cumpleaños en tu casa el sábado. Dibuja un plano para tus amigos y explica cómo se va a tu casa desde la estación.

Remember to use the familiar command form! And if you don't live near a station, give directions from some other obvious landmark.

Exercise 5.15

¡Habla!
Explica cómo se va a:
1. *tu casa*
2. *tu colegio*

Vocabulario 5.1

El ayuntamiento	= the town hall	*Bajar*	= to go down
El banco	= the bank	*Cruzar*	= to cross
El bar	= the bar	*Coger*	= to take
El cine	= the cinema	*Doblar*	= to turn
El estadio	= the sports stadium	*Ir*	= to go
El hotel	= the hotel	*Seguir (i)*	= to continue
El mercado	= the market	*Subir*	= to go up
El restaurante	= the restaurant	*Tomar*	= to take
El supermercado	= the supermarket		
El teatro	= the theatre	*Andando*	= on foot
La cafetería	= the café	*En coche*	= by car
La catedral	= the cathedral	*Eso es*	= that's right
La discoteca	= the discoteque	*Oiga*	= excuse me
La esquina	= the corner (of road)	*Perdone*	= excuse me
La farmacia	= chemist	*¿Por dónde se va a?*	= how do I get to?
La iglesia	= the church	*¿Vale?*	= okay?
La panadería	= the bakery		
La piscina	= the swimming pool	*Despacio*	= slow
La plaza	= the square	*Unos*	= about
La plaza de toros	= the bullring		
La tienda	= the shop	*El norte*	= north
		El sur	= south
		El este	= east
		El oeste	= west

Los países del mundo

We now move on to countries. The vast majority of countries ending in *a* are feminine nouns, with the notable exception of Canada. When learning a country, be sure to learn its gender too. Masculine ones are shown in blue, feminine ones in red.

Norte América
Los Estados Unidos
Canadá

Centroamérica
Méjico
Guatemala
Nicaragua
El Salvador
Honduras
Costa Rica
Panamá

Sudamérica
Venezuela
Colombia
Perú
Bolivia
Ecuador
Paraguay
Uruguay
Chile
Argentina

N.B. *Países de habla hispana*: Spanish speaking countries are shaded red on the maps.

Europa

Because not all of these are immediately recognisable in Spanish, we have given the English names too. We have also listed the appropriate adjectives of nationality, to give you more to learn!

País		Nacionalidad
Inglaterra	= England	inglés
Irlanda	= Ireland	irlandés
Escocia	= Scotland	escocés
Gales	= Wales	galés
Francia	= France	francés
España	= Spain	español
Portugal	= Portugal	portugués
Italia	= Italy	italiano
Alemania	= Germany	alemán
Bélgica	= Belgium	belga
Holanda	= Holland	holandés
Grecia	= Greece	griego
Dinamarca	= Denmark	danés
Noruega	= Norway	noruego
Suecia	= Sweden	sueco
Finlandia	= Finland	finlandés

Exercise 5.16

¡Escucha y habla!
Practica estos diálogos con tu pareja pero cambia el país y la nacionalidad. Luego cambia de papel.

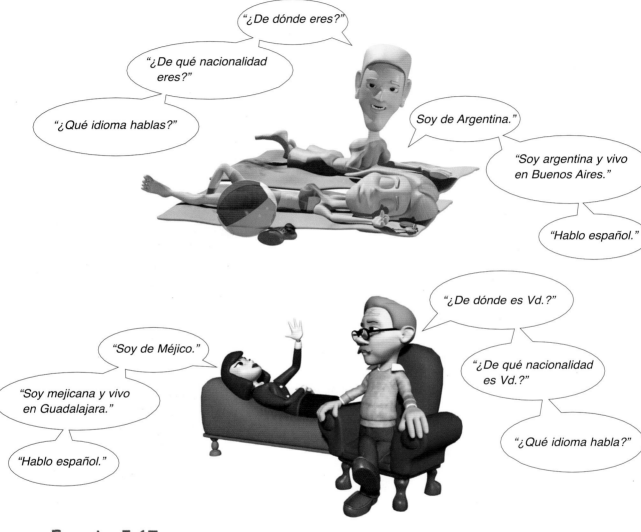

Exercise 5.17

¡Lee y escucha!
¿Qué país es?

1. *Está al sur de Rusia. Es un país muy grande pero no se habla ni inglés ni español.*
2. *Está en el norte de Sudamérica al lado de Colombia. La capital es Caracas. Se habla español.*
3. *Es un país pequeño de Centroamérica entre Panamá y Nicaragua. También se habla español.*
4. *Es un país bastante grande en el sur de Europa donde se habla español.*
5. *Está en el norte de Europa. Es una isla pequeña donde se habla inglés.*
6. *Es un país en el este de Norteamérica donde se habla inglés y también francés.*

N.B. *Se habla* = is spoken

Exercise 5.18

¡Escucha!

¿De dónde eres? Rellena la ficha con: (1) el país de origen; y (2) dónde viven.

Nombre	País de origen	Donde viven
1. Laura		
2. Brita		
3. Damián		
4. Jacqueline		
5. José		
6. Dora		

Exercise 5.19

¡Lee!

Méjico (o México) es un país situado en el extremo meridional de América del norte. Limita al norte con los Estados Unidos; al este con el golfo de México y el Caribe; al sur con Belice y Guatemala y al oeste con el océano Pacífico.

Méjico es el país hispano con mayor número de habitantes y su capital, Ciudad de Méjico, la ciudad más grande del planeta – tiene más de veinte millones de habitantes.

La economía tiene dos sectores principales: la actividad agraria y la minera. México posee una agricultura muy variada: desde los cereales hasta los cultivos tropicales como la caña de azúcar, el café, el cacao, el algodón etc. Es el sexto productor mundial de petróleo y el octavo de gas natural.

El idioma oficial del país es el español y su moneda es el peso mexicano. Si algún día vas a Méjico tienes que visitar el increíble museo de Antropología e Historia en la capital y, en las afueras, las famosas Pirámides de Teotihuacán.

Vocabulario

El extremo meridional = the southern end
Limitar con = to border with

Agrario = agricultural
Minero = mining
Poseer = to have

La caña de azúcar = sugar cane
El cacao = cocoa

El algodón = cotton

La moneda = the currency

Las afueras = the outskirts

Contesta las preguntas:
1. *¿Dónde está Méjico?*
2. *¿Qué país está al norte de Méjico?*
3. *¿Cómo se llama el mar al este de Méjico?*
4. *¿El océano Pacífico está al sur o al oeste de Méjico?*
5. *¿Cuántos habitantes hay en la capital?*
6. *¿Cuáles son las 2 actividades principales del país?*
7. *¿Qué produce Méjico?*
8. *¿Cuál es el idioma oficial?*
9. *¿Cuál es su moneda?*
10. *¿Qué tienes que visitar en las afueras de Méjico?*

Exercise 5.20

¡Escribe!

Los estereotipos

Escribe una frase, como en el ejemplo.

Ejemplo: Los españoles son todos bajos y morenos y tocan la guitarra

Los españoles

1. Los americanos

2. Los holandeses

3. Los chinos

4. Los ingleses

5. Los escoceses

6. Los egipcios

7. Los franceses

8. Los australianos

Exercise 5.21

¡Traduce al español!

1. He's from Bogotá. He's Columbian.
2. She's from Oporto. She's Portugese.
3. We're English. We're from London (*Londres*).
4. The girls are American – from California.
5. Where are you from? (Polite sing.)
6. Where are you from? (Polite pl.)
7. You're from France, aren't you? (Fam. sing.)
8. I'm from Russia. I'm a Russian girl.

Vocabulario	
Japón (masc.)	*japonés*
China (fem.)	*chino*
Rusia (fem.)	*ruso*
Australia (fem.)	*austaliano*
América (fem.)	*americano*
Egipto (masc.)	*egipcio*

El Tiempo

¿Qué tiempo hace hoy?

Notice that when we speak about the weather in Spanish we normally use the 3rd person of the verb *hacer* = to do/make:

Hace buen* tiempo/hace bueno	it's fine weather/it's fine
Hace mal* tiempo/hace malo	it's bad weather/it's horrible
Hace (mucho) calor	it's (very) hot
Hace (mucho) frío	it's (very) cold
Hace sol	it's sunny
Hace viento	it's windy
Hace fresco	it's cool/chilly
Hace 10 grados	it's 10 degrees

* **N.B.** apocopation (chopping off) of final '*o*' before a masculine noun.

But note the following expressions:

Hay niebla	it's foggy
Hay tormenta	it's stormy
Hay escarcha	it's frosty
Hay hielo	it's icy
Llueve (from *llover (ue)*)	it rains
Nieva (from *nevar (ie)*)	it snows

Exercise 5.22

El pronóstico del tiempo
¡Escucha y rellena los huecos!

1. Hoy es el ……………………….. de ………………………..
2. Hace bastante ……………………….. tiempo en España excepto en el ………………………..
3. Allí hace un tiempo ………………………..
4. La temperatura máxima es de ……………………….. grados.
5. En Galicia y Asturias hay ………………………..
6. En el centro de España ……………………….. mucho.
7. Tienes que sacar el ………………………..

Vocabulario

Alcanzar = to reach/go up to (of temperature)	*Las precipitaciones* = rain
El pronóstico del tiempo = weather forecast	*La península* = peninsula
Tiempo soleado = sunny weather	*El paraguas* = umbrella
Tiempo lluvioso = rainy weather	*Fuerte* = strong
Los chubascos = showers	*Los claros* = clear patches

Exercise 5.23

¡Escucha!
El verano en Andalucía
¿Verdad o mentira? Escribe ✓ o ✗ después de cada frase.
1. *En Andalucía en verano hace mucho frío.*
2. *Hace mucho sol.*
3. *A veces la temperatura alcanza los 50 grados.*
4. *Llueve poco.*
5. *Nunca hay tormentas.*
6. *A los turistas extranjeros les gusta el clima en Málaga.*

Vocabulario
La tierra = the ground/earth
Extranjero = foreign
Seco = dry
La tormenta = storm
Hasta (adverb) = even

Exercise 5.24

¡Escucha!
Contesta las preguntas:
El otoño en Galicia
1. *¿Cómo es el tiempo normalmente en Galicia en otoño?*
2. *¿Llueve?*
3. *¿Hace frío?*
4. *¿El clima es igual que en el sur? ¿Por qué (no)?*
5. *En general, ¿Cómo es el clima en Galicia en esta estación del año?*

Vocabulario
Agradable = pleasant
Suave = mild
Igual que = same as

Exercise 5.25

¡Lee y escucha!
El invierno: Un diálogo entre 2 vecinas
Lee y escucha bien la conversación y después escribe un párrafo sobre el clima de Madrid en invierno.

La señora A: *¡Ay, qué frío hace esta mañana! Estamos a 2 grados nada más. Tengo las manos heladas.*

La señora B: *Yo también… pues el hombre del tiempo dice que a lo mejor nieva este fin de semana…*

La señora A: *No creo, pero en la sierra seguro que sí. Para la gente a la que le gusta esquiar hace un tiempo perfecto, ¿no?*

La señora B: *Lo bueno es que aquí en Madrid hace bastante sol en invierno, no como en el norte donde siempre está nublado. Aquí normalmente tenemos un cielo azul, ¿verdad?*

La señora A: *Pues sí, es verdad pero ¡mucho frío, sí que hace!*

La señora B: *Yo de todas formas prefiero el verano.*

Vocabulario

El vecino = the neighbour	*El hombre del tiempo* = the weather man
El cielo = sky	*Lo bueno* = the good thing
Helado = frozen	*La sierra* = the mountains
Esquiar = to ski	*Sí que hace* = that's for sure
Nublado = cloudy	

Exercise 5.26

¡Habla!

Mira el mapa. Con tu pareja prepara un diálogo sobre el tiempo. Uno hace preguntas y el otro contesta.

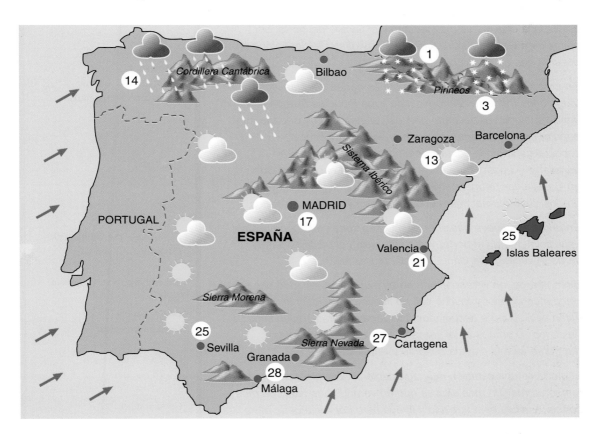

Ejemplo:

1. *¿Qué tiempo hace en Barcelona?*

2. *¿Llueve en Sevilla?*

3. *¿Dónde nieva?*

4. *¿Qué temperatura hace en Madrid?*

5. *¿Qué tiempo hace en el sur?*

Hoy hace bastante mal tiempo en toda la península…

Exercise 5.27

Lee el siguiente artículo sobre el clima en España y contesta las preguntas:

El clima español

En España el clima es muy variado y el tiempo del norte, por ejemplo en Galicia y en Asturias, es muy diferente del tiempo en el sur, o sea en Andalucía.

En invierno hace mucho frío en algunas partes del país, sobre todo en los Pirineos, Sierra Nevada y los Picos de Europa, donde suele nevar bastante. Por eso el esquí es un deporte muy popular en estas montañas. Pero en la parte del sur, especialmente en la costa, suele hacer una temperatura agradable – unos 14 grados – y hace sol. En el centro del país, en Castilla, las temperaturas son muy bajas, algunas veces 0 grados, pero normalmente el cielo es azul y los días soleados.

En primavera llueve bastante en muchas zonas de la península especialmente en el norte, y por esta razón el paisaje es muy verde. A veces hace viento y bastante fresco.

Sin embargo, en verano el tiempo es muy bueno en todo el país. Hace mucho calor y mucho sol, no llueve casi nada y los cielos están casi siempre despejados. Las temperaturas suelen subir hasta los 30 grados en el sur pero a veces hay tormentas. ¡La gente va a la playa a bañarse y refrescarse!

El otoño es una estación muy agradable en España. Las temperaturas son más suaves que en verano y los días son más cortos. A veces está nublado y llueve pero por regla general no hace mal tiempo. ¡Qué gusto!

Vocabulario

O sea = i.e.
Algún, alguna = some
Sobre todo = especially

El paisaje = the countryside
Fresco = fresh, cool

Sin embargo = nevertheless

Casi = almost
Despejado = clear

La playa = the beach

Corto = short
Nublado = cloudy

N.B. *El clima* is masculine, despite the fact that it ends in *-a*. Also note that *la gente* (the people) is *singular*, and is thus followed by a singular verb.

1. *¿Cómo es el clima en España?*
2. *¿Dónde hace mucho frío en invierno?*
3. *¿Por qué es popular el esquí?*
4. *¿Nieva en invierno en las costas del sur de España?*
5. *¿Qué tiempo hace en el sur en invierno?*
6. *¿Cuándo llueve en España?*
7. *¿Cuándo hace calor?*
8. *¿Qué hace la gente en verano? ¿Por qué?*
9. *¿Cómo es el otoño en España?*
10. *¿Qué piensas del clima español?*

Exercise 5.28

¡Escribe y habla!
Escribe un artículo sobre el clima en tu país y preséntalo en clase delante de tus compañeros.
Write an article about the climate in your country and present it to your classmates.

Vocabulario 5. 2

El chubasco	= shower	*Agradable*	= pleasant
El cielo	= sky	*Algún, alguna*	= some
El clima	= climate	*Corto*	= short
El museo	= museum	*Diferente*	= different
El país	= country	*Fuerte*	= strong
El paisaje	= landscape	*Helado*	= frozen
El paraguas	= umbrella	*Increíble*	= incredible
El pronóstico	= forecast	*Lluvioso*	= rainy
El tamaño	= size	*Principal*	= main
El tiempo	= weather	*Soleado*	= sunny
El vecino	= neighbour	*Suave*	= mild
		Variado	= varied
La costa	= the coast		
La gente	= people	*A lo mejor*	= probably
La moneda	= currency	*A veces*	= sometimes
La montaña	= the mountain	*Desde … hasta*	= from … to
La playa	= beach	*Normalmente*	= normally
Las precipitaciones	= rain	*Por eso*	= that's why
La temperatura	= the temperature	*Por regla general*	= as a general rule
		Sin embargo	= however
		Sobre todo	= especially
		¡Qué gusto!	= how nice!

Los deberes

Busca en Internet información sobre cualquier país de habla española y prepara un comentario ilustrado sobre su tamaño, número de habitantes, idioma, clima, etc.

Do a web search to find information about any Spanish-speaking country and prepare an illustrated commentary on its size, population, language, climate etc.

Expectations

At the end of this unit

You should be able to: name common places in town on a map; say where one place is situated in relation to another using common prepositions; ask your way to common places in a town and understand the reply; respond to a request for directions with the correct information; understand how regular imperatives are formed and use them correctly and appropriately; understand simple expressions to describe the weather and enquire what the weather is like in given places; have some knowledge of countries where Spanish is the main language spoken.

You may also be able to: understand and give more complex directions to a specified place; describe more accurately where one place is situated in relation to another; repeat instructions in the first person singular to indicate comprehension; interpret a map to work out directions; make inferences about weather conditions from pictures; find out basic geographical information about selected Spanish-speaking countries.

About the unit

In this final unit you get an opportunity to use the language you have learnt so far to communicate about your hobbies, interests and leisure activities.

New contexts:

- leisure, hobbies, sport, music
- family activities

New language content:

- *preferir* + infinitive
- present continuous tense
- modal verbs *poder, querer*
- interjections
- subject pronouns *él, ella, usted*
- *ir a* + infinitive (immediate future)

Los Deportes

☺ *Me gusta el esquí*

☺☺ *Me gusta mucho la natación*

☹ *No me gusta el fútbol*

☺ *Me gusta también el tenis*

☹ *No me gusta el baloncesto*

☺☺ *Me gusta mucho el patinaje*

☺ *Me gusta también el ciclismo*

☺☺☺ *¡Pero prefiero la vela!*

Vocabulario

El tenis	= tennis	*El rugby*	= rugby
El fútbol	= football	*El patinaje*	= skating
El esquí	= skiing	*El voleibol*	= volley-ball
El atletismo	= athletics	*La natación*	= swimming
El ciclismo	= cycling	*La equitación*	= horse-riding
El footing	= jogging	*La vela*	= sailing
El baloncesto	= basketball	*Los deportes acuáticos*	= water sports
El squash	= squash		

N.B. the word *squash* is pronounced as it is in English.

Jugar (ue) / Practicar

These are the two verbs we need to talk about the sports we do. *Practicar* is used with any sport and always in conjunction with the definite article *el* or *la:*

E.g. *Practico el atletismo y el fútbol.*
     Practico la vela y la natación.

Jugar (ue), as we have already seen, means "to play" and when referring to sports must always be followed by *a* which becomes *al* before a masculine noun. (Most sports are masculine).

E.g. *Juego al tenis, al fútbol y al baloncesto* = I play tennis, football and basketball.
     Juego a las cartas = I play cards.

Exercise 6.1

¡Escucha y empareja los deportes!

1.	Juan	A.	el squash	E.	la natación
2.	David	B.	el atletismo	F.	baloncesto
3.	María	C.	la vela	G.	los deportes acuáticos
4.	Antonio	D.	el ciclismo		
5.	Marisa				

Exercise 6.2

¡Habla!
Trabaja con tu pareja. Pregunta y contesta; luego cambia de papel.

¿Qué deportes practicas?   ¿Cuándo practicas el fútbol/tenis etc.?
¿Dónde juegas?   ¿Qué deportes te gustan más?
¿Con quién juegas?   ¿Por qué?
¿Hay algún deporte que no te gusta?

Exercise 6.3

¡Escribe!
Inventa unas frases, como en el ejemplo:

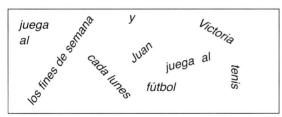

Juan juega al fútbol cada lunes y Victoria juega al tenis los fines de semana.

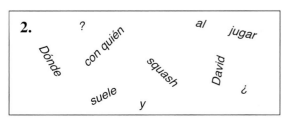

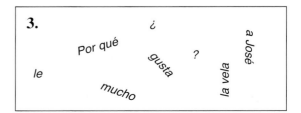

Exercise 6.4

¡Escucha!
1. *¿Cuándo practica Verónica la vela?*
2. *¿Juega José mucho al fútbol?*
3. *¿Nunca juega Dolores al baloncesto?*
4. *¿Qué hacen Dolores y Juan los lunes y los miércoles?*
5. *¿Qué hacen los chicos y las chicas los sábados?*

Exercise 6.5

¡Escribe!
Cambia el orden de las palabras para que la frase tenga sentido:
1. *gusta, a, la, José, le, lectura, no.*
2. *música, Victoria, a, gusta, le, la, pop.*
3. *Juan, no, a, el, le, gusta, teatro.*
4. *la, mucho, le, música, no, Dolores, clásica, gusta, a.*

☹ *No me gusta*

☹☹ *¡No me gusta nada!*

☹ *No me gusta mucho*

☺☺ *¡Prefiero!*

Exercise 6.6

¡Escucha!
Escucha y rellena la ficha.
¿Qué deportes practicas?

Nombre	**Deportes/pasatiempos**	
	☺☺	☹☹
Lolita *Eduardo* *Felipe* *Cristina* *Elena*		

Exercise 6.7

¡Lee y escucha!

La familia Martínez

En esta familia hay 5 personas y todos son muy deportistas. El padre, que se llama Carlos, es un hombre muy activo – en verano después del trabajo juega al tenis tres veces por semana en el club de tenis de Tarragona. Es su deporte favorito y se le da bastante bien. En invierno suele hacer footing para mantenerse en forma.

Su mujer, Carmen, es profesora de guitarra y va a clase de gimnasia con sus amigas los lunes, los miércoles y los viernes. A veces acompaña a su marido a hacer footing.

Sus tres hijos – Susana, Maribel y Daniel van al mismo colegio donde practican la gimnasia, el atletismo y el baloncesto. A Daniel le gusta mucho el baloncesto y juega para el equipo del colegio. A las dos hermanas les gusta mucho la natación pero no hay piscina en el colegio por lo que tienen que ir a un polideportivo en el centro del pueblo. Son muy buenas nadadoras.

Los fines de semana, cuando hace buen tiempo, todos van al mar a practicar la vela.

Vocabulario

Para (+ infin.)	= in order to	*El equipo*	= the team
Mantenerse en forma	= to keep fit	*El polideportivo*	= the sports centre
Acompañar	= to accompany	*El nadador*	= the swimmer
Mismo	= same	*Deportista*	= sporty

Contesta las preguntas:
1. ¿A la familia Martínez le gustan los deportes?
2. ¿Qué deportes practica el padre?
3. ¿Cuándo va a clase de gimnasia Carmen?
4. ¿Cuál es el deporte favorito de Daniel?
5. ¿Qúe deporte prefieren Susana y Maribel?
6. ¿Hay piscina en el colegio?
7. ¿Adónde van para la clase de natación?
8. ¿Qué hacen todos los fines de semana cuando hace buen tiempo?

Exercise 6.8

¡Escribe!

Cambia el orden de las palabras para que la frase tenga sentido.

1.   *José, fútbol, juega, al.*
2.   *día, Felipe, practica, cada, atletismo, el.*
3.   *chicas, siempre, las, guapas, al, juegan, baloncesto.*
4.   *inteligentes, al, nunca, los, juegan, chicos, fútbol.*
5.   *al, España, los, jugamos, en, nosotros, golf, semana, de, fines.*

Exercise 6.9

¡Escribe!

1.   My brother plays rugby at the weekend.
2.   My friends always play basketball on Sunday.
3.   My sister usually does athletics on Tuesdays.
4.   We never play football at school.
5.   My father sometimes plays squash after work.

Me gusta + infinitive

Notice that when we say what we like, dislike or prefer *doing* in our free time, in Spanish we must use the INFINITIVE after *me gusta*.

Ejemplo:

☺	*Me gusta* **esquiar**	= I like skiing.
☺	*Nos gusta* **practicar** *deportes*	= We like doing sport.
☹	*A ella no le gusta* **leer**	= She doesn't like reading.
☹☹	*A ellos no les gusta nada* **ir** *al teatro*	= They don't like going to the theatre at all.

¿Qué prefieres hacer?

¡Habla!

Practise a conversation with your partner, using some of the activities below.

Vocabulario

Bailar = to dance
Charlar con amigos = to chat with friends
Escribir cartas = to write letters
Escuchar música = to listen to music
Hablar por teléfono = to talk on the phone
Hacer vela = to go sailing
Ir al cine = to go to the cinema
Ir a la discoteca = to go to the disco
Ir a fiestas = to go to parties
Ir de tiendas/de compras = to go shopping

Leer revistas = to read magazines
Mandar e-mails = to send e-mails
Montar en bici(cleta) = to ride a bike
Nadar = to swim
Navegar por internet = to surf the web
Patinar = to skate
Relajarse = to chill out/relax
* *Salir con amigos* = to go out with friends
** *Tocar la guitarra* = to play the guitar
Ver telenovelas = to watch soaps

---

* Irreg. 1st person: *salgo*

** To play a sport = *jugar (ue) + al* (most sports are masculine!). To play a musical instrument = *tocar*.

Exercise 6.10

¡Lee y traduce al inglés!
1.   *Me gusta mucho ir a fiestas los sábados.*
2.   *Me encanta charlar con mis amigos por teléfono.*
3.   *No me gusta nada escribir cartas.*
4.   *Prefiero mandar e-mails.*
5.   *Me gusta esquiar en los Pirineos porque es chulo.*
6.   *¿Te gusta ir de tiendas?*
7.   *A mi padre le gusta jugar al golf.*
8.   *A mi madre le gusta ver telenovelas.*
9.   *¡A mí me gusta pasarlo bien!*
10. *Preferimos el fútbol al tenis.*

N.B. There are several ways of saying e-mails in Spanish:
Los e-mails
Los correos electrónicos
Los emilios (slang)

Exercise 6.11

¡Habla!
Pregunta a tu pareja lo que le gusta o no le gusta hacer en su tiempo libre, qué prefiere hacer y por qué.
Luego cambia de papel.

Ejemplo: *"¿Qué te gusta hacer en tus ratos libres?"*
               "Me gusta practicar la vela o ir al cine, pero no me gusta nadar."
               "¿Qué prefieres hacer?"
               "Creo que prefiero practicar la vela."
               "¿Por qué?"
               "Porque me encanta; ¡es divertido!"

A few useful expressions might be :

Es chulo	= it's cool!
Es divertido	= it's fun!
Es genial	= it's great!
Es guay	= it's great/super/cool!
Es un rollo	= it's a bore!
Me encanta	= I love!
Me chifla	= I'm crazy about!
Pasarlo bomba	= to have a great time.

Ejemplo: *¡Me gusta pasarlo bomba!* = I like having a great time.
               Nos encanta el fútbol = we love football.

Exercise 6.12

¡Escribe!
Traduce al español
1.   What do you like doing in your free time?
2.   I like swimming and dancing.
3.   She likes reading.
4.   We love water sports.
5.   They prefer going to the disco.

Exercise 6.13

Escribe frases completas para describir tus pasatiempos con una palabra o palabras de cada columna.

Normalmente	Me gusta	Salir	Revistas
A veces	No me gusta	Escuchar	Cartas
Por la tarde	Prefiero	Practicar	Vela
Los sábados	Me encanta	Ir	Al ajedrez
		Jugar	A mis amigos
		Escribir	El squash
		Telefonear	A la discoteca
		Hacer	Al tenis
		Ver	Con amigos
		Leer	Música clásica
			La tele

Exercise 6.14

¡Lee y escribe!
Una carta de tu amigo

You have just received this letter from your Spanish penfriend, Carlos. Unfortunately, your dog got hold of it and by a complete coincidence, the teeth-marks went through all the expressions about likes and dislikes! Try to fill in the gaps and then translate the letter.

Me llamo _____ y voy a hablar de
mi familia y de mis amigos. A mí me
_____ mucho los deportes. Sobre todo
gusta la natación, pero no me _____
el rugby. ¡Es una barbaridad! A mis padres
_____ gusta mucho ir a los toros
pero a mi hermano, Imanol, no _____
gusta la corrida. Tengo muchos amigos.
Mi mejor amiga se llama Carolina y _____
gusta mucho bailar en la disco. A _____
me gusta bailar también. Tengo un
amigo que se llama Manuel. A Manuel le
_____ practicar la vela. A mi no me
_____ los deportes acuáticos. ¿Qué _____
gusta hacer en tu tiempo libre?

¡Escríbeme pronto!

Saludos de Carlos

Exercise 6.15

¡Escucha!
Rellena la tabla.
¿Qué les gusta hacer en su tiempo libre y cuándo?

Nombre	☺ ¿Qué les gusta?	¿Cuándo?
1. Teresa		
2. José María		
3. Manolo		
4. Laura		
5. Elena		

Vocabulario 6.1

El equipo	= the team	*La actividad*	= activity
El polideportivo	= the sports centre	*La equitación*	= horse-riding
El/la nadador(a)	= the swimmer	*La música*	= music
		La natación	= swimming
El atletismo	= athletics	*La vela*	= sailing
El baloncesto	= basketball		
El ciclismo	= cycling	*Bailar*	= to dance
Los deportes acuáticos	= water sports	*Charlar*	= to chat
El esquí	= skiing	*Hacer vela*	= to go sailing
El footing	= jogging	*Mandar e-mails*	= to send e-mails
El fútbol	= football	*Montar en bicicleta*	= to ride a bicycle
El pasatiempo	= hobby	*Nadar*	= to swim
Los deportes	= sport(s)	*Navegar por internet*	= to surf the web
El patinaje	= skating	*Navegar*	= to sail
El rugby	= rugby	*Patinar*	= to skate
El squash	= squash	*Practicar*	= to do (a sport)
El tenis	= tennis	*Salir*	= to go out
El voleibol	= volley-ball	*Tocar*	= to play (an instrument)

Me gusta navegar por internet…

The present continuous tense

We shall now look at another form of the present tense, called the present continuous tense. This is the tense we use when we say what we *are doing* at this moment, rather than simply what we *do* generally. E.g. I am learning Spanish; I am reading the book; I am laughing at the jokes.

This tense is formed with the present tense of the verb *estar* plus the present participle (*el gerundio*, the '-ing' bit in English). Note: we use **ESTAR** in Spanish – we can NEVER use *ser*.

This is all great if we know how to form the present participle of a verb, which we don't. So now we need to learn how to do that.

AR Verbs

The present participle of *AR* Verbs is formed by removing the *ar* and adding *ando* to the stem:

Estudiar → *estudiando* = studying

	Singular	**Plural**
1st person	*Estoy estudiando*	*Estamos estudiando*
2nd person	*Estás estudiando*	*Estáis estudiando*
3rd person	*Está estudiando*	*Están estudiando*

E.g. *Estoy estudiando español.*

ER and IR Verbs

The present participle of *ER* and *IR* verbs is formed by removing the *er* or *ir* and adding *iendo* to the stem:

Comer → *comiendo* = eating
Escribir → *escribiendo* = writing

	Singular	**Plural**
1st person	*Estoy comiendo*	*Estamos comiendo*
2nd person	*Estás comiendo*	*Estáis comiendo*
3rd person	*Está comiendo*	*Están comiendo*

	Singular	**Plural**
1st person	*Estoy escribiendo*	*Estamos escribiendo*
2nd person	*Estás escribiendo*	*Estáis escribiendo*
3rd person	*Está escribiendo*	*Están escribiendo*

E.g. *Mi padre está comiendo.*
Mis amigos están escribiendo las cartas.

N.B. In the -*er* and -*ir* verbs something peculiar happens when there is a vowel left once we have removed the -*er* or -*ir* ending of the infinitive. The *iendo* becomes *yendo*.

Ejemplo:	*Le-er*	*leyendo*	reading
	Cre-er	*creyendo*	believing
	Constru-ir	*construyendo*	building

N.B. One verb which is very rarely found in the present continuous tense is the verb *ir* = to go.

E.g. *¿Adónde vas?* = where **are** you **going**?
Voy al colegio = I **am going** to school.

En Casa

¡Lee y escucha!

Mamá:	*"¿Me ayudas en la cocina, por favor, Pablo?"*
Pablo:	*"Pero mamá, estoy estudiando. Tengo un examen mañana...."*
Mamá:	*"Niñas, ¿qué estáis haciendo?"*
Niñas:	*"Estamos viendo un programa muy interesante en la tele..."*
Mamá:	*"¿Y papá, qué está haciendo?"*
Ana:	*"Creo que está leyendo un libro en el salón..."*
Mamá:	*"¡Vaya familia!"*

> **Vocabulario**
> *Ayudar* = to help
> *Un examen* = examination
> *¡Vaya ...!* = what a ...!

Exercise 6.16

¡Lee y escribe en inglés!

1. *La chica está escribiendo una carta.*
2. *El hombre está trabajando en una oficina.*
3. *Los turistas están visitando la catedral.*
4. *Los chicos están viendo la televisión.*
5. *Las chicas están escuchando música.*

Exercise 6.17

¡Escribe!

Give the gerund (present participle) of the following verbs:
1. *fumar*
2. *comer*
3. *vivir*
4. *nadar*
5. *beber*

Exercise 6.18

¡Escribe!

1. The teacher is speaking in Spanish.
2. The boys are eating chocolate in the sitting room.
3. What are you doing? (Familiar, sing.)
4. We are writing in English.
5. I am listening to the radio in my bedroom.

Reflexive Verbs

As we have already seen with the simple present, the reflexive pronoun comes in front of the verb, e.g. *me lavo; me baño*. But in the present continuous there are two possibilities for the position of the pronoun. It can precede the verb or be attached to the end of the present participle, in which case an accent must be added.

Me estoy lavando	*or*	*estoy lavándome*	I am washing myself, etc.
Te estás lavando		*estás lavándote*	
Se está lavando		*está lavándose*	
Nos estamos lavando		*estamos lavándonos*	
Os estáis lavando		*estáis lavándoos*	
Se están lavando		*están lavándose*	

Exercise 6.19

Escribe el presente continuo (las dos formas) de:

1. *ducharse*
2. *levantarse*

Exercise 6.20

¡Lee y escribe!

La familia Muñoz

Son las siete y media de la mañana. El señor Muñoz ya está arreglándose para el trabajo – está lavándose y afeitándose mientras que su mujer se está peinando en el dormitorio. Miguel, el hijo mayor, está levantándose de la cama pero tiene mucho sueño. Su hermana, Carolina, está preparándose para el colegio: así que se está duchando en el cuarto de baño. Ángel se está despertando muy despacio – ¡porque no le gusta mucho ir al colegio!

Vocabulario	
Arreglarse	= to get ready
Prepararse	= to get ready
Afeitarse	= to shave
Tener sueño	= to be sleepy (literally: to have sleep)
Mientras que	= while

1. *Busca todos los verbos reflexivos en el presente continuo.*
2. *Escríbelos y luego escribe el verbo otra vez, cambiando la posición del pronombre.*
3. *Traduce la frase al inglés.*

Ejemplo:

1. *El señor Muñoz está arreglándose.*
2. *El señor Muñoz se está arreglando.*
3. Señor Muñoz is getting ready.

Radical Changing verbs – Present Continuous

1. **AR and ER verbs**

When we form the present participle from verbs that are normally radical changing in the simple present tense, no radical change will occur, because the root vowel is not being stressed.

Simple present		Present participle	
Empezar (ie)	emp**ie**zo	empezando	= beginning
Pensar (ie)	p**ie**nso	pensando	= thinking
Jugar (ue)	j**ue**go	jugando	= playing
Volver (ue)	v**ue**lvo	volviendo	= returning

2. **IR verbs**

However, with *IR* radical changing verbs, whether single or double vowel change, a **single** vowel change will occur (E → I and O → U) in the present participle. This change occurs not because the root vowel is being stressed as in the simple present, but because the next syllable contains the letters -*ie*. Now don't tell me this book is for dummies; this is the real thing!

Simple present		Present participle	
Vestirse (i)	me v**i**sto	vistiéndome	= getting dressed
Dormir (ue)	d**ue**rmo	durmiendo	= sleeping

At this stage we need not worry too much about this category of radical changing verbs, because you will be studying them in more detail in later books.

Exercise 6.21

¡Lee y traduce!
1. Estoy empezando a leer un libro muy interesante.
2. ¿Qué estás pensando?
3. Los niños están jugando en el parque.
4. En este momento mi padre está volviendo de la oficina.
5. Nos estamos acostando porque tenemos sueño.

Exercise 6.22

¡Lee y traduce al inglés!
1. "¿Qué estás haciendo?"
2. "Estoy vistiéndome en mi dormitorio".
3. "¿Qué está haciendo Juan?
4. "Está durmiendo en el sofá".

Exercise 6.23

¡Escribe!
Escribe el presente continuo (el verbo completo) de:
1. empezar (ie)
2. jugar (ue)
3. vestirse (i)
4. dormir (ue)

Exercise 6.24

¡Escribe o habla!
¿Qué están haciendo?
Ejemplo: El rey y la reina están bailando.

Exercise 6.25

¡Escucha!

"Oye, ¿Qué estás haciendo?"

Escucha estas conversaciones telefónicas y escribe lo que están haciendo:

1. Jaime
2. Javier
3. Marisa

4. Ester
5. Miguel
6. Concha

Exercise 6.26

¡Habla!

Pregunta a tu pareja: "¿Qué estás haciendo?" Tu pareja inventa una respuesta.

Ejemplo: *"¿Qué estás haciendo?"*

                "Estoy escuchando música."

Un juego

¡Habla!

Trabaja con tu pareja. Tú haces un mimo y preguntas a tu pareja: "¿Qué estoy haciendo?" Tu pareja tiene que adivinar lo que estás haciendo. Luego cambia de papel.

Ejemplo: *"¿Qué estoy haciendo?"*

                "Estás bebiendo una coca cola."

                "No".

                "Estás bebiendo un vaso de leche."

                "Sí"

¿Qué estoy haciendo?

Querer (ie)

Now you might *want* to do something ! So now we need to learn a pretty important verb – the verb 'to want'. And here it is:

Querer (ie) = to want	Singular	Plural
1st person	quiero	queremos
2nd person	quieres	queréis
3rd person	quiere	quieren

As you can see, it's another one of those radical changing verbs. As far as you're concerned at the moment, this verb is followed by the infinitive.

E.g. *Yo quiero aprobar mis exámenes* = I want to pass my exams.

    El profesor no quiere suspender a sus alumnos = the teacher doesn't want to fail his pupils.

    Nosotros queremos ir al cine = we want to go to the cinema.

Remember that 'qu' in Spanish is pronounced as a 'k' apart from in one word, *el squash,* which is pronounced as it is in English.

Exercise 6.27

Escucha y empareja la actividad con la persona adecuada.
¿Qué quieres hacer?

1.	Sergio	a)	*quiere ir de compras*
2.	Patricia	b)	*quiere ir al cine pero no puede*
3.	Silvia	c)	*quiere jugar al tenis*
4.	Juanjo	d)	*quiere salir con sus amigos pero no puede*
5.	Gabriel	e)	*quiere hacer vela*

Exercise 6.28

¡Escribe!
1. *Escribe 10 cosas que quieres hacer este fin de semana y di por qué.*
2. *Escribe en español las frases siguientes:*

a) I want to ride my bike.
b) Do you want to dance? (Familiar, sing.)
c) She wants to go out.
d) We want to chat.
e) You want to go to the party, don't you? (Familiar, pl.)
f) They want to watch the television.
g) What do you want to do? (Polite, sing.)

> **Vocabulario**
> *Me gustaría* = I would like
> *¡Qué pena!* = What a pity!
> *Que te mejores* = I hope you feel
> better soon
> *¡No fastidies!* = you're joking!

Exercise 6.29

¡Lee y escribe en inglés!

Pepe: "Mamá, quiero ir a la discoteca con mis amigos este sábado.
Maria: Yo también quiero ir con Beatriz a una fiesta.
Mamá: Y tú, Pablo, ¿qué quieres hacer?
Pablo: Pues, papá y yo queremos ir al estadio a ver al Real Madrid.
Mamá: ¿Pero no queréis ir a cenar a casa de la abuela?
Todos: Por favor, mamá, ¡no fastidies!

Poder (ue)

The final verb which we are going to look at in this unit is the verb 'to be able' often translated as 'can'. The infinitive is *poder* and yes, it is radical changing!

Poder (ue) = to be able

Singular		**Plural**
1st person	*puedo*	*podemos*
2nd person	*puedes*	*podéis*
3rd person	*puede*	*pueden*

This verb, like *querer*, is always followed by the infinitive.
E.g. *Puedo jugar a los deportes en mi colegio* = I am able to/I can play sports in my school.
E.g. *Puedes aprender el español fácilmente, si estudias* = you are able to/you can learn Spanish easily if you study.

> **En España**
> *¡Querer es poder!* = where there's a will there's a way!

Exercise 6.30

¡Escribe!
Traduce al español

1. I can't play tennis.
2. Can you go out? (Familiar, pl.)
3. She cannot telephone.

4. We can eat in a restaurant.
5. They can study in the library.
6. You can go sailing in Spain. (Polite, pl.)

Exercise 6.31

As we have seen, the subject pronouns are not usually used in Spanish except for emphasis or contrast.

Ejemplo :   *El lunes **yo** voy a la piscina pero **tú** vas al estadio.*
                 ***Ella** practica el tenis pero **él** practica el fútbol.*

¡Traduce al español!

1. On Tuesday I go to school, but you (polite, sing.) go to the bank.
2. On Wednesday, we go out but they stay at home.
3. On Thursday you (familiar, sing.) play golf and he plays basketball.
4. On Friday she goes shopping but you (familar, pl.) watch the television.

Exercise 6.32

¡Lee!

> **Vocabulario**
> *Quedarse en casa* = To stay at home

Málaga, 22 de noviembre

¡Hola!

¿Qué tal? Yo me llamo Jorge y tengo 14 años. Soy malagueño y vivo con mi familia en un pueblecito en las afueras de Málaga. Mi abuela también vive con nosotros. Somos 5 personas en total, mis padres, mi hermana (que se llama Maribel) y yo, y mi abuela claro. Vivimos en una casa bastante grande en el campo y por eso tenemos muchos animales: dos perros grandes (pastores alemanes) cuatro gatos y una tortuga. A mí me encantan los animales. ¿A tí te gustan los animales?

Te voy a hablar un poco sobre mi rutina diaria y mis pasatiempos. Voy a un instituto mixto en el centro de Málaga así que tengo que levantarme bastante pronto, sobre las 7 y media, de lunes a viernes.¿A qué hora te levantas tú normalmente? Suelo desayunar poco: un zumo de naranja y unas galletas. Salgo de casa a las 8 y cojo el autobús que me deja cerca del instituto. Las clases empiezan a las 8.30 pero suelo charlar con mis amigos en el patio antes de entrar. Normalmente termino las clases a las dos de la tarde pero los jueves por la tarde tenemos clase de gimnasia, fútbol y balconcesto así que no llego a casa hasta las 6 y pico.

Los sábados no hay clase, ¡menos mal! y puedo levantarme tarde. Me gusta mucho salir con mis amigos. A veces vamos a un bar a charlar y a tomar algo; otras veces vamos al cine o a una discoteca. En verano vamos a la playa a nadar y a hacer windsurfing. Aquí en Málaga hace muy buen tiempo. ¿Qué tiempo hace donde vives tú? Este sábado vamos a ir a un concierto de música pop.¡Genial!

Bueno, nada más por hoy. Escríbeme pronto y háblame de tu familia, tu colegio y tus pasatiempos.

Un abrazo de tu amigo: Manolo

Exercise 6.33

¡Escribe!
Escribe una carta a Manolo, contestando a sus preguntas y dando información sobre ti.

Exercise 6.34

¡Lee o escucha!

Me llamo Gloria. Tengo 15 años. Vivo en las Islas Canarias con mis padres y mi hermana menor. En mi tiempo libre me gusta leer revistas y ver telenovelas. Soy muy deportista – juego al baloncesto y al tenis. Me encantan la gimnasia y la natación

Mi nombre es Alberto. Soy de Costa Rica. Tengo 16 años. En mi familia somos 3 hermanos - todos chicos! A mí me gusta mucho tocar la guitarra – me chifla la música pop. Los sábados voy a la discoteca a bailar con mis amigos. A veces voy a conciertos.

Me llamo Raquel. Tengo 24 años. Soy española – de Madrid. Tengo una hermana mayor. Yo trabajo como profesora en una escuela primaria. Los fines de semana me gusta ir con amigos a fiestas. ¡Lo pasamos bomba!

Soy Marcelo. Tengo 14 años. Vivo con mis padres en Buenos Aires, en Argentina. Somos familia numerosa, 3 chicas y 3 chicos. Muchos hermanos, ¿verdad? En mis ratos libres me encanta jugar con el ordenador y mandar e-mails. También suelo hablar mucho por teléfono con mis amigos. Me gusta mucho montar en bici y nadar.

¡Escribe!
¿Verdad o mentira?
Pon ✓ o ✗ después de cada frase. Si la frase es falsa, corrígela.

<u>Gloria</u>

1. *Gloria es española.*
2. *Tiene una hermana mayor.*
3. *Le gusta ver telenovelas.*
4. *No es nada deportista.*

<u>Alberto</u>

5. *Alberto es español.*
6. *Tiene 3 hermanas.*
7. *Le gusta tocar la guitarra.*
8. *Los domingos va a la discoteca.*

<u>Raquel</u>

9. *Raquel es de Madrid.*
10. *Trabaja como secretaria.*
11. *Le gusta salir con amigos los sábados y los domingos.*
12. *Lo pasan muy bien.*

<u>Marcelo</u>

13. *Marcelo es argentino.*
14. *Hay 9 personas en su familia.*
15. *En su tiempo libre le gusta esquiar.*
16. *Le gusta mucho la natación.*

Immediate future

We already know how to use the verb *ir* to say where we go or are going, so now we can very easily say what we are going to do in the future by just adding '*a*' + the infinitive. So here's the golden rule:

IR + *a* + infinitive = to be **going to do** something.

Ejemplo: *Esta tarde voy a salir con mis amigos* =
             This afternoon I'm going to go out with my friends.

N.B. If the infinitive is a reflexive verb, we must remember to change the reflexive pronoun to agree with the subject of the sentence.

Ejemplos: *Voy a levantarme tarde.*
              Vas a levantarte a las 8.
              Va a bañarse en la piscina.
              Vamos a bañarnos en el mar.
              Vais a acostaros a las 10.
              Van a acostarse temprano.

> **Vocabulario**
> *Esta tarde* = this afternoon
> *Mañana* = tomorrow
> *Pasado mañana* = the day after tomorrow
> *Este fin de semana* = this weekend
> *El próximo fin de semana* = next weekend
> *La semana que viene* = next week

Exercise 6.35

¡Lee y traduce al inglés!

1. *Mañana voy a escribir una carta a mi amigo.*
2. *El sábado próximo tú vas a ir a una fiesta, ¿verdad?*
3. *Usted va a pasarlo bien este fin de semana.*
4. *Mi madre va a ir de compras esta mañana.*
5. *Vamos a ver una película esta noche.*
6. *Vais a montar en bici pasado mañana.*
7. *Van a visitar España la semana que viene.*
8. *Vds. van a aprender español.*

Exercise 6.36

¡Escribe!
¿Cómo se dice en español?

1. This afternoon I'm going to do my homework.
2. Tomorrow she is going to play basketball.
3. We're going to go shopping on Saturday.
4. They are going to watch a football match *(un partido de fútbol)*.
5. What are you going to do this afternoon? (Familiar, sing.)
6. I'm going to have a shower.
7. Are you going to go to bed? (Familiar, pl.)
8. Are you going to get up late? (Polite, sing.)

Exercise 6.37

¡Escribe!
Mira los dibujos y rellena los huecos con el infinitivo correspondiente.
¿Qué vas a hacer mañana?

Bailar   *Escribir*   *Comprar*   *Nadar*   *Mirar*   *Estudiar*   *Cenar*   *Orar*

1.   *Voy a* ....
     a mi abuela.

2.   *Voy a* ....
     en la iglesia.

3.   *Voy a* ....
     en la piscina.

4.   *Voy a* ....
     la corrida.

5.   *Voy a* ....
     en la discoteca.

6.   *Voy a* ....
     en el restaurante.

7.   *Voy a* ....
     en el colegio.

8.   *Voy a* ....
     las verduras.

Exercise 6.38

¡Escucha!

Nombre	¿Qué hacen normalmente?	¿Qué van a hacer?
Mónica		
Mari Carmen		
Isabel		
Ana y Rosita		
Paloma		

Exercise 6.39

¡Habla!

1.   *Prepara un pequeño discurso de lo que vas a hacer este fin de semana y preséntalo a tus compañeros. Tienes que decir cuándo exactamente y por qué.*

2.   *Entrevista a tu pareja y luego cambia de papel.*

Ejemplo: *¿Qué vas a hacer esta tarde?*
               ¿Qué vas a hacer mañana?
               ¿Qué vas a hacer este fin de semana?
               ¿Qué vas a hacer el sábado por la mañana?
               ¿Qué vas a hacer en verano?
               ¿Qué vas a hacer en Navidad?
               ¿Qué vas a hacer en Semana Santa?
               ¿Qué vas a hacer durante las vacaciones?

Vocabulario 6.2

Afeitarse	= to shave	*El examen*	= exam
Arreglarse	= to get ready	*La fiesta*	= party
Ayudar	= to help	*El patio*	= courtyard, playground
Dar	= to give	*La revista*	= magazine
Orar	= to pray		
Prepararse	= to get ready	*A diario*	= every day
Quedarse en casa	= to stay at home	*Contigo*	= with you
Querer	= to want	*Fuera*	= outside
Tener sueño	= to be sleepy	*Menos mal*	= thank goodness
Tomar algo	= to have a drink	*Pasado mañana*	= the day after tomorrow
		Próximo	= next

Los deberes

Prepara un folleto con tus actividades fuera del colegio.

Mis actividades

En mi tiempo libre juego al baloncesto y al tenis pero lo que más me gusta es la natación. Voy a la piscina todos los días antes del colegio.

Juego al fútbol y al voleibol y me chifla el esquí. Vivimos cerca de los Pirineos así que suelo esquiar bastante en invierno con mis amigos. Hago gimnasia y baloncesto en el colegio pero no me gustan mucho. Pero soy miembro de un club de atletismo y eso sí que me gusta mucho. Soy bastante deportista, entonces me gustan todos los deportes.

En mi tiempo libre toco la guitarra.

Me encanta la música, y me gusta bailar y escuchar música. Hago patinaje, que me gusta mucho y luego como vivo cerca del mar

practico deportes acuáticos como el windsurfing. Los fines de semana, cuando hace buen tiempo, todos van al mar a practicar la vela. A mí me gusta bailar también. Me encanta ir con mis amigos a la discoteca. Me encanta la lectura – leo sobretodo libros de aventuras. También me gusta relajarme, leer revistas y navegar por Internet. ¡Me encanta mi tiempo libre!

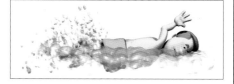

mucho. Pero soy miembro de un club de

Expectations

At the end of this unit

You should be able to: read short texts about leisure activities, deducing meanings and using a dictionary where necessary; understand information about future plans from passages made up of familiar words; say what you are doing at the moment, what you are going to do, and describe what other people are doing; speak with reasonably accurate pronunciation and intonation; speak and write about what leisure activities you like and dislike, giving reasons.

You may also be able to: understand longer passages and conversations, deducing the meaning of new words; take part in structured conversations about plans for the weekend, showing some creativity and fluency; write about your leisure interests, enhancing the language with suitable adverbs and adjectives; use a dictionary and other reference materials to check accuracy and understanding; write paragraphs, largely from memorised language, but incorporating language from different contexts.

At this stage we bid you farewell – see you in Book 2!

Vocabulario: español-inglés

A = to, at
A diario = daily
A eso de = around (time)
A la sal = cooked in salt
A la una = at one o'clock
A las dos = at two o'clock
A lo mejor = probably
A mano… = on the…hand side
A mi juicio = in my judgement
A veces = sometimes
Abrazo, el = hug, embrace; *un abrazo* = with best
    wishes
Abril = April
Abrir = to open
Abuela, la = grandmother
Abuelo, el = grandfather
Aburrido = boring
Academia, la = academy
Acento, el = accent
Acompañar = to accompany
Acordarse (ue) = to remember
Acostarse (ue) = to go to bed
Actividad, la = activity
Activo = active
Actuar = to perform
Acuático = aquatic
Acuerdo, el = agreement
Acuesto: see *Acostarse (ue)*
Adecuado = adequate, appropriate
Adiós = goodbye
Adivinar = to guess
Adjetivo, el = adjective
¿Adónde? = where to?
Afeitarse = to shave
Aficionado, el = fan, supporter
Afueras, las = outskirts
Agenda, la = diary, address book
Agosto = august
Agradable = pleasant
Agrario = agricultural
Agricultura, la = agriculture
Agua (fem.), el = water
Ahora mismo = right now
Ahora = now
Ajedrez, el = chess
Ajo, el = garlic

Al ajillo = cooked in garlic
Al fin de = at the end of
Al lado de = next to
Alcanzar = to reach, go up to
Alemán = German
Alemán, el = German (the language)
Alemania (fem.) = Germany
Alfabeto, el = alphabet
Alfombra, la = carpet
Algo = something
Algo, tomar = to have a drink
Algodón, el = cotton
Algún, alguna = some
Algunas veces = sometimes
Allá = there (in the distance)
Allí = there (quite near)
Almorzar (ue) = to have lunch
Almuerzo, el = lunch
Alto = tall
Alumno/a, el/la = pupil
Ama (fem.) de casa, el = housewife
Amarillo = yellow
América (fem.) = America
Americano = American
Amiga, la = friend (fem.)
Amigo, el = friend (masc.)
Añadir = to add
¡Anda! = come on, come off it!
Andando = on foot
Animal, el = animal, pet
Antes de (+ infin.) = before -ing
Antiguo = old, ancient
Anorak, el = anorak
Antipático = horrible, unkind
Antropología, la = anthropology
Año, el = the year
Año que viene, el = next year
Apartado postal (apdo. Postal), el = PO box
Aparte (adverb) = apart
Apellidarse = to be called (a surname)
Apellido, el = surname
Apodo, el = nickname
Aprender = to learn
Aprobar (ue) = to pass (an examination)
Aquí = here
Araña, la = spider

Árbol, el = tree
Argentina (fem.) = Argentina
Argentino = Argentinian
Armario, el = wardrobe, cupboard
Arreglar = to fix
Arreglarse = to get ready
Arriba = above, upstairs
Arte, el = art
Artículo, el = article
Así = like that
Así que = so, so then
Asignatura, la = subject (school)
Aspirina, la = aspirin
Atletismo, el = athletics
Aula (fem.), *el* = classroom
Australia (fem.) = Australia
Australiano = Australian
Autobús, el = bus
Ayuntamiento, el = town hall
Ayer = yesterday
Ayudar = to help
Azúcar, el/la = sugar
Azul = blue
Baca, la = roof-rack
Bailar = to dance
Bajar = to go down
Bajo = short (height), low
Bajo (adverb) = below
Baloncesto, el = basketball
Balonmano, el = handball
Banco, el = bank
Bañarse = to have a bath, to swim in the sea
Bañera, la = bath
Baño, el = bathroom
Bar, el = bar
Barato = cheap
Barbaridad, la = barbarism
Bastante = quite, enough
Bastar = to be enough, sufficient
Batido, el = milkshake
Beber = to drink
Bebida, la = drink
Belén, el = nativity scene
Belga = Belgian
Bélgica (fem.) = Belgium
Berato = cheap
Besugo, el = sea bream
Biblioteca, la = library
Bici, la (abbreviation) = bike
Bicicleta, la = bicycle

Bien = well, good (when asking how someone is)
Biología, la = Biology
Blanco = white
Bocadillo, el = sandwich
Bocata, el = baguette
Boli, el (abbreviation) = pen
Bolígrafo, el = pen, biro
Bollo, el = bun
Bonito = pretty, nice-looking
Brújula, la = compass
Bueno (*buen* before masc. sing. noun) = good
Buenas noches = good night
Buenas tardes = good afternoon
Buenos días = good day, hello
Burro, el = donkey
Buscar = to look for
Butaca, la = armchair
Caballo, el = horse
Cabeza, la = head
Cacao, el = cocoa
Cada = each, every
Caer = to fall
Café (*con leche*), *el* = (white) coffee
Cafetería, la = café
Calamares a la romana, los = squid cooked in batter
Calcetines, los = socks
Calculadora, la = calculator
Calibre, el = calibre
Caliente = hot
Callarse = to be quiet
Calle, la = street
Calor, el = heat
Cama, la = bed
Camino, de = on the way
Cambiar = to change
Cambia de papel = swap around, change roles
Campeón, el = champion
Campo, el = countryside, field
Caña de azúcar, la = sugar cane
Canadá (masc.) = Canada
Canarias, las = Canaries
Cancela, la = iron gate
Cantina, la = canteen, dining room
Capilla, la = chapel
Capital, la = the capital (city)
Cara, la = face
El Caribe (masc.) = The Caribbean
Caribeño = (from the) Caribbean
Cariñoso = loving, affectionate

Carne, la = meat, flesh
Carpeta, la = file, folder
Carretera, la = road
Carta, la = letter, playing card
Casa, la = house
Casi = almost
Castaño = chestnut-coloured
Castellano, el = Castilian, Spanish (the language)
Castillo, el = castle
Catalán = Catalan
Catedral, la = cathedral
Catorce = fourteen
Cava, el = champagne
Ceja, la = eye-brow
Celebrar = to celebrate
Cena, la = dinner
Cenar = to have one's evening meal
Centro, el = centre
Centroamérica (fem.) = Central America
Cerca (de) = close, near (to)
Cerdo, el = pork
Cereales, los = cereals
Cerradura, la = lock
Cerveza, la = beer
Chabola, la = shack
Chalet, el = a detached villa
Chapuza, la = odd job
Chaqueta, la = jacket
Charlar = to chat
Chica, la = girl
Chico, el = boy
Chiflar = to be crazy about (works like *gustar*)
Chile (masc.) = Chile
Chileno = Chilean
China (fem.) = China
Chino = Chinese
Chocolate, el = chocolate
Chorizo, el = spicy red salami sausage
Chubascos, los = showers
Chulo = cool (colloquial)
Chupar = to suck
Ciclismo, el = cycling
Cielo, el = sky, heaven
Cien(to) = hundred
Ciencias, las = the sciences; Science
Cigarillo, el = cigarette
Cinco = five
Cincuenta = fifty
Cine, el = cinema
Cinta, la = the tape

Ciudad, la = the city
Clara, la = shandy
Claro = of course, clear, bright
Claros, los = clear patches
Clase, la = class, classroom
Clásico = classical
Clima, el = climate
Club, el = club
Coca cola, la = coke
Cocer (ue) = to cook
Coche, el = car
Cochinillo, el = suckling pig
Cocido, el = stew
Cocina, la = kitchen
Cocinar = to cook
Cocinero, el = cook
Coger = to take
Colacao = a popular chocolate drink
Cole, el = school (shortened form)
Colegio, el = school (primary or independent secondary)
Colombia (fem.) = Columbia
Colombiano = Columbian
Color, el = colour
Columna, la = column
Comedor, el = dining room
Comentario, el = commentary
Comenzar (ie) = to begin
Comer = to eat
Comida, la = food, meal, lunch
Como = as, like
¿Cómo? = how?
¿Cómo es? = what is….like?
¿Cómo son? = what are….like?
¿Cómo te llamas? = what is your name? (informal)
¿Cómo se llama usted? = what is your name? (formal)
Cómodo = comfortable
Compact disc, el = CD, CD player
Compañero/a, el/la = companion
Comparar = to compare
Completar = to complete
Completo = complete
Compra, la = shopping
Comprar = to buy
Comprender = to understand
Con = with
Con gas = fizzy
Concierto, el = concert

Conejo, el = rabbit
Congelador, el = freezer
Conocer (1st pers. sing = *conozco*) = to know (a person or place)
Conserje, el = caretaker
Consistir en = to consist of
Construir = to build
Contento = content, happy
Contestar = to answer
Contigo = with you
Continuo = continuous
Conversación, la = conversation
Corbata, la = cravat, neck-tie
Cordero, el = lamb
Corona, la = crown
Correcto = correct
Corregir (i) = to correct
Correo electrónico, el = e-mail
Correos = post office
Correr = to run
Correspondiente = corresponding
Corrida de toros, la = bullfight
Corrida, la = bullfight
Cortar = to cut
Corto = short (length)
Cosa, la = thing
Costa, la = coast
Costa Rica (fem.) = Costa Rica
Creer = to think, believe
Cruzar = to cross
Cuaderno, el = exercise book
Cuadrilla, la = team
Cuadro, el = painting
¿Cuál? = which? what? (interrog.)
¿Cuándo? = when? (interrog.)
Cuando = when
¿Cuánto/s? = how much, many?
Cuarenta = forty
Cuarto de baño, el = bathroom
Cuarto = fourth
Cuarto, el = quarter
Cuatro = four
Cuatrocientos = four hundred
Cubano = Cuban
Cuece: see *cocer (ue)*
Cuidado, el = care
Cultivo, el = crop
Cumpleaños, el = the birthday
Cumplir = to reach the age of
Curiosidad, la = curiosity

Curso, el = (school) year
Danés = Danish
Dar = to give
De = of, from
¡De acuerdo! = agreed!
De camino = on the way
De media = on average
De nada = not at all, it's my pleasure
De primer plato = as a first course
De segundo = as a second course
De vez en cuando = from time to time
Debajo de = under
Deberes, los = homework
Debería = I/he/she ought
Decidir = to decide
Décimo = tenth
Decir (i); 1st person singular *digo* = to say
Dedo, el = finger
Dejar = to leave, allow, drop off
Del: de + el = of the
Delante de = in front of
Deletrear = to spell out
Delgado = thin
Demasiado = too
Deporte, el = sport
Deportes acuáticos, los = water sports
Deportes, los = sports, games
Deportista = sporty
Deportivo = sporty
Derecho = right
Desayunar = to have breakfast
Describir = to describe
Descripción, la = description
Descubrir = to discover
Desde luego = of course
Desde = from
Despacio = slow
Despejado = clear
Despertarse (ie) = to wake up
Después de = after
Después = afterwards
Detrás de = behind
Dí (from *decir*) = say
Día, el = the day
Diálogo, el = dialogue
Diario = daily
Dibujar = to draw
Dibujo, el = art, picture, drawing
Diccionario, el = dictionary
Dice: see *decir*

Diciembre = December
Dieciséis = sixteen
Diecisiete = seventeen
Diecinueve = nineteen
Dieciocho = eighteen
Diente, el = tooth
Dieta, la = diet
Diez = ten
Diferente = different
Dinamarca (fem.) = Denmark
Dirección, la = address
Director, el = headteacher (male)
Directora, la = headteacher (female)
Disciplinado = disciplined
Discoteca, la = disco
Discurso, el = speech
Divertido = fun, funny, amusing
Dividido = divided
Dividir = to divide
Doblar = to turn
Doce = twelve
Domicilio, el = residence
Domingo = Sunday
Donde = where
¿Dónde? = where?
Donut, el = donut
Dorado = golden, gold-coloured
Dormir (ue) = to sleep
Dormitorio, el = bedroom
Dos = two
Doscientos = two hundred
Ducha, la = shower
Ducharse = to have a shower
Durante = during
Durar = to last
Economía, la = economy
Ecuador (masc.) = Ecuador
Edad, la = age
Edificio, el = building
Educación física, la = P.E. (physical education)
Educación Secundaria Obligatoria, la = compulsory secondary education (i.e. secondary school)
Educado = polite, cultured
Ejemplo, el = example
Ejercicio, el = exercise
Egipcio = Egyptian
Egipto (masc.) = Egypt
El = the (masculine singular)
Él = he

El que = (that) which
El Salvador (masc.) = El Salvador
Elegir = to choose
Ella = she
Ellos/as = they
Emilio, el (slang) = e-mail
Emparejar = to match up
Empezar (ie) = to start, begin
Empujar = to push
En = in, on
En coche = by car
En general = generally
En mi opinión = in my opinion
En punto = on the dot, o'clock
En seguida = at once
En total = in total
Encantar = to love (works like *gustar*)
Encerrar (ie) = to shut, lock up
Encontrar (ue) = to meet, to find
Encuesta, la = survey
Enero = January
Enfrente (de) = opposite (to)
Ensalada, la = salad
enseñar = to teach
Entonces = then, so then
Entrar = to enter, go in
Entre = between
Entrevista, la = interview
Entrevistar = to interview
Equilibrado = balanced
Equipo, el = team, equipment
Equitación, la = (horse) riding
Era (imperfect tense of *ser*) = he/she/it was
Eres (from *ser*) = you (sing.) are
Es (from *ser*) = he/she/it is
Es decir = that is to say, i.e.
Escarcha, la = frost
Escocés = Scottish
Escocia (fem.) = Scotland
Escolar (adj.) = (of a) school
Escribir = to write
Escuchar = to listen
Escuela, la = school
Ese, esa, esos, esas = that, those (demonstrative adjective)
Ése, ésa, ésos, ésas = that, those (demonstrative pronoun)
ESO = compulsory secondary education
Eso es = that's right
Espada, la = sword

España (fem.) = Spain
Español = Spanish
Español, el = Spanish (language)
Especial = special, fussy
Especialmente = especially
Espectáculo, el = spectacle, show
Espejo, el = mirror
Esquí, el = skiing
Esquiar = to ski
Esquina, la = corner (street/road)
Estación, la = station, season
Estadio, el = stadium
Estados Unidos, los = USA
Estantería, la = bookcase
Estar = to be
Estar despejado = to be clear
Estar nublado = to be cloudy
Este, el = east
Éste/a/o = this (one)
Estereotipo, el = stereotype
Esto = this (thing)
Estuche, el = pencil-case
Estudiar = to study
Estudiante, el/la = student
Estupendo = superb/great
Ética, la = ethics
Euro, el = euro
Examen, el = exam
Exactamente = exactly
Excepto = except (for)
Expedido (esped.) = issued
Explicar = to explain
Explosivo, el = explosive
Extranjero = foreign
Extranjero, el = foreigner
Extremo meridional, el = the southern end
Fácil = easy
Fácilmente = easily
Falda, la = skirt
Fallas, las = Festivals celebrated in Valencia in March in which they burn 'Fallas' or cardboard effigies
Falso = false
Familia, la = family
Famoso = famous
Fanta = Fanta (popular brand name for fizzy drinks)
Fantástico = fantastic
Farmacia, la = chemists
Fastidio, el = nuisance, boredom

Fatal = awful
Favorito = favourite
Febrero = February
Fecha, la = date
Feliz = happy
Fenomenal = brilliant
Feria, la = fair, market, show
Ficha, la = form, record-card
Fideo, el = noodle
Fiesta, la = the party, festival
Filete, el = fillet
Fin de semana, el = weekend
Fin, el = end
Final de, el = the end of
Finlandés = Finnish
Finlandia (fem.) = Finland
Física, la = physics
Flan con nata, el = crème caramel with cream
Flor, la = flower
Florido = flowery
Folleto, el = brochure
Footing, el = jogging
Forma, la = shape, form
Francés = French
Francés, el = French (language)
Francia (fem.) = France
Frase, la = sentence
Frecuencia, con poca = rarely
Fregadero, el = sink
Fregar (ie) = to scrub (wash dishes)
Fresco = fresh, cool
Frío, hacer = to be cold
Fruta, la = fruit
Fue (from *ser*) = he/she/it was
Fuera = outside
Fuerte = strong
Fumar = to smoke
Furioso = angry, furious
Fútbol sala, el = indoor (5-a-side) football
Fútbol, el = football
Galaxia, la = galaxy
Galés = Welsh
Gales (masc.) = Wales
Galleta, la = biscuit
Garbanzo, el = chickpea
Gas, el = gas
Gato, el = cat
General = general
Genial = great
Gente, la (used in singular) = people

Geografía, la = geography
Gibraltareño = from Gibraltar
Gimnasia, la = gym
Golf, el = golf
Golfo, el = the gulf
Goma, la = rubber
Gordo = fat
Gorro, el = cap, beret
Gracias = thank you, thanks
Grado, el = degree
Grande = big
Granja, la = farm
Grecia (fem.) = Greece
Griego = Greek
Gris = grey
Gritar = to yell
Guapo = handsome, pretty
Guatemala (fem.) = Guatemala
Guay = super, great, cool (informal)
Guitarra, la = guitar
Gustar = to please
Gusto, el = taste, pleasure, liking for
Habitación, la = room
Habitante, el/la = inhabitant
Hablar = to speak
Hablar por teléfono = to speak on the telephone
Hace (mucho) calor = it's (very) hot
Hace (mucho) frío = it's (very) cold
Hace buen tiempo, hace bueno = it's fine weather
Hace fresco = it's cool, chilly
Hace mal tiempo, hace malo = it's bad weather
Hace sol = it's sunny
Hace viento = it's windy
Hace x grados = it's x degrees
Hacer (irreg.) = to do, make
Hacer vela = to go sailing
Hacerse (irreg.) = to become
Hamaca, la = hammock
Hambre (fem.), *el* = hunger
Hámster, el = hamster
Harto, estar = to be fed up
Hasta = until, even
Hasta la vista = see you later
Hasta luego = see you later
Hay = there is, there are
Hay escarcha = it's frosty
Hay hielo = it's icy
Hay niebla = it's foggy
Hay que = one has to
Hay tormenta = it's stormy

Helado = frozen
Helado, el = ice-cream
Helicóptero, el = helicopter
Hermana, la = sister
Hermanastra, la = step-sister
Hermanastro, el = step-brother
Hermano, el = brother
Hielo, el = ice
Hierba, la = grass
Hija, la = daughter
Hija única, la = only child (female)
Hijo, el = son
Hijo único, el = only child (male)
Hispano = Hispanic, Spanish
Historia, la = history, story
Hola = hi, hello
Holanda (fem.) = Holland
Holandés = Dutch
Hombre, el = man
Honduras (masc.) = Honduras
Hora, la = hour, time
Horario, el = timetable
Horno, el = oven
Horrible = horrible
Hospital, el = hospital
Hotel, el = hotel
Hoy = today
Hoy en día = nowadays
Hueco, el = blank, gap
¡Id! (from *ir*) = go!
Idioma, el = language
Ídolo, el = idol
Iglesia, la = church
Igual que = same as
Ilustrado = illustrated
Imagen, la = image, picture
Imbécil = stupid
Imperativo, el = imperative
Importante = important
Increíble = incredible
Indicar = to indicate, point out
Infinitivo, el = infinitive
Indio = Indian
Información, la = information
Informática, la = ICT
Inglaterra (fem.) = England
Inglés = English
Inglés, el = English (the language)
Inhumano = inhuman
Instituto, el = school (secondary)

Instrucción, la = instruction
Inteligente = intelligent
Intentar = to try (attempt)
Interesante = interesting
Inventar = to invent
Investigar = to research, find out
Invierno, el = Winter
Ir (irreg.) = to go
Ir a (+ infin.) = to be going to do (simple future)
Ir de tiendas, ir de compras = to go shopping
Irlanda (fem.) = Ireland
Irlandés = Irish
Isla, la = isle, island
Italia (fem.) = Italy
Italiano = Italian
Izquierda = left
Jabón, el = soap
Jamón, el = ham
Japón (masc.) = Japan
Japonés = Japanese
Jardín, el = garden
Jarra, la = jar
Joven = young
Juego, el = game
Jueves = Thursday
Jugar = to play
Julio = July
Junio = June
Juntos = together
Justo = just, right
Kilómetro, el = kilometre
La = the (fem. sing.)
Laboral = working (adj.)
Laboratorio, el = laboratory
Lado, el = side
Lámpara, la = lamp
Lápiz, el = pencil
Largo = long
Latín, el = Latin
Lavabo, el = basin
Lavadora, la = washing-machine
Lavaplatos, el = dishwasher
Lavar = to wash
Lavarse = to wash oneself, to get washed
Le = him, to him, to her
Leche, la = milk
Lectura, la = reading
Leer = to read
Lejos (de) = far (from)
Lengua, la = language

Lenguado, el = sole (fish)
León, el = lion
Les = to them
Levantarse = to get up
Libre = free
Libro, el = book
Lidiar = to bullfight
Ligero = light (adj.)
Limitar con = to border with
Limón, el = lemon
Limpiarse los dientes = to brush one's teeth
Literatura, la = literature
Llamarse = to be called
Llegar = to arrive
Llevar = to carry, wear
Llevarse bien con = to get on well with
Llover (ue) = to rain
Llueve = it rains
Lluvioso = rainy
Lo = it (direct object pronoun)
Lo bueno = the good thing
Lo malo = the bad thing
Lo peor = the worst thing
Lo siento = I'm sorry
Localidad, la = location, town
Londres = London
Los = the (masc. pl.); them (direct object pronoun)
Lubina, la = sea bass
Luego = then
Lunes = Monday
Luz, la (pl. *luces*) = light
Madrastra, la = step-mother
Madre, la = mother
Madrileño = from Madrid
Madrugada, la = dawn, early morning
Magnífico = great, superb
Malagueño = from Málaga
Malo (*mal* before masc. sing. noun) = bad
Mamá = mum, mummy
Mandar = to order, send
Mano, la = hand
Mantenerse en forma = to keep fit
Mantenimiento, el = maintenance, up keep
Mantis religiosa, la = praying mantis
Mañana = tomorrow
Mañana, la = the morning
Mapa, el = map
Mar, el = sea
Marido, el = husband

Mariscos, los = shellfish
Marrón = brown
Martes = Tuesday
Mártir, el/la = martyr
Martirizar = to torture, martyr
Marzo = March
Más = more, most, plus (+)
Mascota, la = pet
Matador, el = the bullfighter who kills the bull
Matar = to kill
Matemáticas, las = maths
Máximo = top, highest
Mayo = May
Mayor = older, oldest, bigger, biggest
Mazapán, el = marzipan
Me = me, to me, myself
Me chifla = I love, I'm mad about
Me gustaría = I would like (conditional tense)
Médico, el = doctor
Mejicano = Mexican
Medio = half
Méjico (masc.) = Mexico
Mejor = better, best
Mencionar = to mention
Menor = younger, smaller
Menos = less, minus (-)
¡Menos mal! = thank goodness!
Menos cuarto = quarter to
Mentir (ie) = to tell a lie
Mentira, la = lie
Mercado, el = market
Merendar (ie) = to have a snack, to have tea
Meridional = southern
Merienda, la = afternoon snack
Merluza, la = hake (fish)
Mes, el = month
Mesa, la = table
Mesita de noche, la = bedside table
Meter = to put
Metro, el = metre; the underground
  (train system)
Mexicano, mejicano = Mexican
Mi(s) = my
Miedo, el = fear
Mientras que = while
Miércoles = Wednesday
Mil = thousand
Millón, el = million
Mimo, el = mime
Mina, la = mine

Mineral = mineral
Minería, la = mining
Minero = mining (adj.)
Minuto, el = minute
Mirar = to look at, watch
Misa, la = mass
Mismo = same
Mixto = mixed (adj.)
Mochila, la = rucksack, school-bag
Moderno = modern
Momento, el = moment
Moneda, la = currency
Montaña, la = mountain
Montar en bici(cleta) = to ride a bike
Morado = purple
Moreno = dark (colour)
Muchas gracias = thank you very much
Mucho = much, many, a lot
Muebles, los = furniture
Mujer, la = woman, wife
Muleta, la = cape
Multiplicado = multiplied
Multiplicar = to multiply
Mundial = of the world (adj)
Mundo, el = world
Municipal = municipal
Museo, el = museum
Música, la = music
Muy = very
Muy buenas = hi there
Nacer = to be born
Nacimiento, el = birth
Nació = (he/she) was born
Nacionalidad, la = nationality
Nada = nothing
Nadador, el = swimmer
Nadar = to swim
Naranja = orange (the colour)
Naranja, la = orange (the fruit)
Nariz, la = nose
Nata, la = cream
Natación, la = swimming
Natural = natural
Navegante, el = sailor
Navegar = to sail; to surf (e.g. the internet)
Navidad, la = Christmas
Necesario = necessary
Negro = black
Nevar (ie) = to snow
Nevera, la = fridge

Ni…ni = neither…nor
Nicaragua (fem.) = Nicaragua
Niebla, la = fog
Nieta, la = grand-daughter
Nieto, el = grandson
Nieva: see *nevar (ie)*
Nieve, la = snow
Ninguno (*ningún* before masc. Sing. noun) = no, not any
Niña, la = girl, child (female)
Niño, el = boy, child (male)
No = not, no
¡No fastidies! = you must be joking!
No importa = it doesn't matter
Noche, la = night
Nochebuena, la = Christmas Eve
Nochevieja, la = New Year's Eve
Nocilla, la = a type of chocolate spread
Nombre, el = the name
Normalmente = normally
Norte, el = north
Noruega (fem.) = Norway
Noruego = Norwegian
Nos = us, to us, ourselves
Nosotros/as = we
Novecientos = nine hundred
Noveno = ninth
Noventa = ninety
Novia, la = girlfriend
Noviembre = November
Novio, el = boyfriend
Nublado = cloudy
Nuestro = our
Nueve = nine
Nuevo = new
Número, el = the number
Numeroso = numerous
Nunca = never
O = or
O sea = i.e./ that's to say
Obligatorio = compulsory
Océano, el = ocean
Ochenta = eighty
Ocho = eight
Ochocientos = eight hundred
Octavo = eighth
Octubre = October
Oeste, el = west
Oficial = official
Oficina de turismo, la = tourist information office

Oficina, la = office
Oiga = excuse me
Ojo, el = eye
Olvidar = to forget
Once = eleven
Opinar que = to think that
Optativo = optional
Optimista = optimistic, hopeful
Orar = to pray
Orden, el = order
Ordenador, el = computer
Oreja, la = ear
Origen, el = origin
Oro, el = gold (the metal)
Os = you, to you, yourselves
Otoño, el = Autumn
Otra vez = again, another time
Otro = other
Pacífico, el = Pacific
Padrastro, el = step-father
Padre, el = father; parent
Paella, la = paella
Pagano = pagan
Página, la = page
País, el = country
Paisaje, el = countryside, landscape
Pájaro, el = bird
Palabra, la = word
Pan, el = bread
Panadería, la = bakery
Panamá (fem.) = Panama
Papá = Dad, Daddy
Papel, el = paper; piece of paper
Para = for
Para (+ infin.) = in order to
Para chuparse los dedos = delicious (lit. to suck one's fingers)
Paraguas, el = umbrella
Paraguay (masc.) = Paraguay
Parecer = to appear, seem; *me parece que* = I think that
Parecido = similar
Pared, la = wall (of a building)
Pareja, la = pair, partner
Parque, el = park
Párrafo, el = paragraph
Parrilla, la = grill
Partido, el = match, game, team
Pasado mañana = the day after tomorrow
Pasar lista = to take the register

Pasarlo bien = to have a good time
Pasarlo bomba = to have a great time
Pasatiempos, los = hobbies
Pasta, la = pasta; cash (slang)
Pastor alemán, el = German shepherd
Patatas fritas, las = chips
Patata, la = potato
Patinaje, el = skating
Patinar = to skate
Patio, el = the courtyard, playground
Patriótico = patriotic
Patrona, la = patron
Pavo, el = turkey
Peatón, el = pedestrian
Pedir (i) = to ask for
Peinarse = to comb one's hair
Película, la = film
Pelirrojo = redhead, ginger
Pelo, el = hair
Pena, la = sorrow, trouble, pain
Península, la = the peninsula (e.g. Spain &
    Portugal)
Pensar (ie) = to think
Pequeño = small
Perder (ie) = to lose
Perdone = excuse me
Perezoso = lazy
Perfecto = perfect
Periódico, el = newspaper
Permitir = to allow
Pero = but
Perro, el = dog
Persona, la = person
Personaje, el = celebrity, important person,
    character
Perú (masc.) = Peru
Pesado = annoying
Pescado, el = fish
Pesimista = pessimistic
Peso, el = weight; peso (unit of currency in S.
    America)
Petróleo, el = oil, petroleum
Pez, el (plural peces) = fish
Pico, y = and a bit
Piel, la = skin
Pienso: see Pensar (ie)
Pintado = painted
Pintor, el = painter
Pirámide, la = pyramid
Piscina, la = swimming pool

Piso, el = floor, flat
Pizza, la = pizza
Pizarra, la = blackboard
Planeta, el = planet
Plano, el = plan, map
Planta, la = floor (of apartment building)
Plata, la = silver (the metal)
Plateado = silver (the colour)
Plato, el = dish, course
Playa, la = beach
Plaza de toros, la = bullring
Plaza, la = square (of a town)
Poblado = bushy
Pobre = poor
Poco = a little (amount)
Poder (ue) = to be able
Polideportivo, el = sports centre, sports hall
Pollo, el = chicken
Poner = to put
Ponerse = to become
Pop = pop (short for popular)
Popular = popular
Por = by, for, along, through; (+ infin.) in order to
¿Por dónde se va a? = how do I get to?
Por ejemplo = for example
Por eso = that's why
Por este motivo = for this reason
Por favor = please
Por primera vez = for the first time
¿Por qué? = why?
Por regla general = as a general rule
Porque = because
Portugal (masc.) = Portugal
Portugués = Portuguese
Poseer = to have, possess
Posición, la = position
Póster, el = poster
Postre, el = dessert, pudding
Practicar = to practise, do, play (e.g. a sport)
Precipitaciones, las = rain
Preferido = favourite
Preferir (ie) = to prefer
Pregunta, la = question
Preguntar = to ask (a question)
Preparar = to prepare
Prepararse = to prepare oneself, get ready
Presentar = to present
Presente = present (adj.)
Presente, el = present (tense)
Prima, la = cousin (female)

Primario = primary
Primavera, la = Spring
Primer plato, el = first course (of meal)
Primero (*primer* before masc. sing. noun) = first
Primo, el = cousin (male)
Principal = main
Privado = private
Problema, el = problem
Producir = to produce
Productor, el = producer
Profesor, el = teacher (male)
Profesora, la = teacher (female)
Programa, el = programme
Pronombre, el = pronoun
Pronóstico del tiempo, el = weather forecast
Pronto = quickly, promptly
Pronunciar = to pronounce
Provincia, la = province
Próximo = next
Proyector, el = projector
Pueblecito, el = small town
Pueblo, el = town, village
Puede: see *poder (ue)*
Puerta, la = door
Pues = well, um, then
Pupitre, el = desk
Que = that (after a verb)
¿Qué? = what?
¡Que aproveche! = *bon apetit*, enjoy your meal!
¡Qué gusto! = how nice!
¿Qué hay? = how's it going?
¡Qué miedo! = how scary!
¡Qué pena! = what a shame, pity!
¡Qué pesado! = what a pain!
¡Qué suerte! = how lucky!
¿Qué tal? = how are you?
¡Que te mejores! = I hope you get better!
¡Qué va! = no way, come off it!
Que viene = that is coming, next
Quedarse en casa = to stay at home
Querer (ie) = to want
Querer es poder = 'where there's a will, there's a way'
Queso, el = cheese
Quien = who (relative pronoun)
¿Quién? = who?
Quiero: see *Querer (ie)*
Química, la = chemistry
Quince = fifteen
Quinientos = five hundred

Quinto = fifth
Quitarse la ropa = to get undressed
Quizá(s) = perhaps, maybe
Radio, la = radio
Rato, el = (short) time
Ratón, el = mouse
Rayo, el = lightning
Razón, la = reason
Real = real, royal
Real Madrid, el = Real Madrid (a football team)
Recibir = to receive
Recreo, el = break
Recto = straight
Redondo = round
Reflexivo = reflexive
Refrescarse = to cool down
Refresco, el = soft drink
Regalo, el = present
Región, la = region
Regla, la = ruler, rule
Regresar = to return
Regular = so so; not bad
Reina, la = queen
Relajarse = to 'chill out', relax
Religión, la = Religious Studies, R.E.
Rellenar = to fill in
Reloj, el = watch, clock
Renfe = Spain's national railway network
Repaso, el = revision
Representado = represented
Responsable = responsible
Respuesta, la = the answer
Restaurante, el = restaurant
Revista, la = magazine
Rey, el = king
Rezar = to pray
Riquísimo = delicious
Rizado = curly
Rojo = red
Rollo, el = mess, bore
Ropa, la = clothes
Rosa = pink
Rosado = rosé (wine)
Rotulador, el = marker pen
Rubio = blonde, fair-skinned
Rudo = rough
Rugby, el = rugby
Rusia (fem.) = Russia
Ruso = Russian
Rutina, la = routine

Sábado = Saturday

Saber = to know

Sabroso = tasty

Sacapuntas, el = pencil sharpener

Sacar = to take out, take (photos)

Sal, la = salt

Sala, la = room

Sala de estar, la = living room

Sala de profesores, la = staff room

Salchichón, el = spicy salami sausage

Salir (1st pers. sing. = *salgo*) = to go out

Salón, el = living room

Saludos = best wishes, greetings

Sano = healthy

Santo, el = saint

Se = one, himself/herself/themselves

Se habla = is spoken

Se me da(n) bien = I'm good at

Se me da(n) fatal = I'm bad at

Se(p)tiembre = September

Seco = dry

Secretaria, la = secretary

Sector, el = sector

Seguida, en = in a moment, right away

Seguir (i) (1st person sing. = *sigo*) = to follow, continue

Según = according to

Segundo = second

Segundo plato, el = main course (of meal)

Seguro = sure, certain

Seis = six

Seiscientos = six hundred

Semáforo, el = traffic-light

Semana Santa, la = Holy Week (Easter)

Semana, la = week

Señor = Mr, sir

Señora = Mrs, madam

Señores X, los = Mr and Mrs X

Señorita = miss

Sentarse (ie) = to sit down

Sentido, el = sense

Sentido, tener = to make sense

Septiembre = September

Séptimo = seventh

Ser fuerte en = to be good at

Ser = to be

Sesenta = sixty

Setecientos = seven hundred

Setenta = seventy

Sexto = sixth

Si = if

Sí = yes

Siempre = always

Sierra, la = mountain range

Siete = seven

Sigo: see *Seguir (i)*

Siguiente = following

Silla, la = chair

Simpático = kind, nice

Sin embargo = however

Sin gas = without gas, still (non-fizzy)

Sitio, el = place

Situado = situated

Sobre todo = especially

Sobre = above, on top of, on, about (of time)

Sofá, el = sofa

Sois (from *ser*) = you (pl.) are

Sol, el = sun

Soleado = sunny

Soler + infinitive = to be accustomed to do something – to 'normally' do

Sólo = only

Solucionar = to solve

Somos (from *ser*) = we are

Son (from *ser*) = they are; equals (=)

Sopa de fideos, la = noodle soup

Sopa, la = soup

Soy (from *ser*) = I am

Squash, el = squash

Su(s) = his/her/its/their (+ your, in polite form)

Suave = mild

Subir = to go up

Subrayar = to underline

Sucio = dirty

Sudamérica (fem.) = South America

Suecia (fem.) = Sweden

Sueco = Swedish

Suelo, el = floor, flat

Suelo: see *soler (ue)*

Sueño, tener = to be sleepy

Suficiente = sufficient, enough

Supermercado, el = supermarket

Sur, el = south

Surf, el = surf

Suspender = to fail (an examination)

Tabla, la = plank, board, chart

Tablón, el = notice-board

Tamaño, el = size

También = also, too

Tan = so

Tanto = so much
Tapar = to cover
Tarde = late
Tarde, la = afternoon, early evening
Te = you, to you/ yourself
Teatro, el = theatre
Techo, el = ceiling
Tecnología, la = Technology
Tejado, el = roof
Tele, la = TV
Telefonear = to telephone
Telefónico = telephonic
Teléfono, el = telephone
Telenovela, la = TV soap-opera
Televisión, la = television
Temperatura, la = temperature
Temprano = early
Tender (ie) = to hang out
Tener (ie) (1ˢᵗ person sing. = *tengo*) = to have, hold, consider; be (x years old)
Tener que (+ infin.) = to have to, be obliged to
Tener sueño = to be tired/sleepy
Tengo: from *tener* = I have
Tenis, el = tennis
Tercero = third
Terminar = to finish
Ternera, la = beef, veal
Terraza, la = terrace
Testigo, el = witness
Tí (used after prepositions) = you, yourself
Tía, la = aunt
Tiempo, el = time, weather
Tiempo lluvioso = rainy weather
Tiempo soleado = sunny weather
Tiene(s): from *tener (ie)*
Tienda, la = shop
Tierra, la = ground, earth
Tijeras, las = scissors
Tímido = timid
Tinto = red (wine)
Tío, el = uncle
Típico = typical
Tipo, el = type
Título, el = title, heading
Tocar = to play (a musical instrument)
Todavía = still, yet
Todo = every, all
Todo el mundo = everybody
Todo recto = straight ahead
Tomar = to take (to have of meals)

Tomar algo = to have a drink
Tomar la alternativa = to become a matador
Torcer (ue) (1st person sing. = *tuerzo*) = to twist, turn
Torear = to bullfight
Tormenta, la = storm
Toro, el = bull
Toros, los = bullfight
Tortilla, la = omelette
Tortuga, la = tortoise
Tostadas, las = toast
Tostado = toasted
Tostador, el = toaster
Trabajador = hardworking
Trabajar = to work
Trabajo, el = work
Tradición, la = tradition
Traducir = to translate
Treinta = thirty
Tres = three
Trescientos = three hundred
Tropical = tropical
Tú = you (sing.)
Tu(s) = your
Turista, el/la = tourist
Turrón, el = nougat
Tutoría, la = tutorial
Un, una = a
Un abrazo = with best wishes
Único = only
Universidad, la = university
Uno = one
Unos = some, a few; about
Uruguay (masc.) = Uruguay
Usted (Vd.), ustedes (Vds.) = you (polite form)
Usted verá = you will see
Útil = useful
Utilizar = to use
Va (from *ir*) = he/she/it goes
Vaca, la = cow
Vacaciones, las = holidays
Vago = lazy
¿Vale? = ok?
Válido (val.) = valid
Valiente = brave, strong
Vamos (from *ir*) = we go; let's go
Variado = varied
Vario = assorted, various
Vas (from *ir*) = you (sing.) go
Vaso, el = glass

Vaya/vayan (from ir) = go!

¡Vaya! = what a shame!

Vd., ud., usted = you (polite singular)

Vds., uds., ustedes = you (polite plural)

Ve (from ir) = go!

Veces: (pl. of *vez*)

Vecino, el/la = neighbour

Vegetariano = vegetarian

Veinte = twenty

Vela, la = sailing

Vencido, el = the loser

Vender = to sell

Venezuela (fem.) = Venezuela

¡Venga! = come on!

Ventana, la = window

Ver = to see

Verá (from ver) = he/she/it will see

Verano, el = summer

Verbo, el = verb

Verdad, la = truth

Verdadero = true

Verde = green

Verduras, las = vegetables, greens

Vestíbulo, el = hall

Vestirse (i) = to get dressed

Vez, la (pl.: *veces*) = time (occasion)

Vía, la = way

Viaje, el = journey

Vida, la = life

Vídeo, el = video

Viejo = old

Viento, el = wind

Viernes = Friday

Vino, el = wine

Visitar = to visit

Vista, la = sight, glance

Visto: see *vestirse (i)*

Vivir = to live

Voleibol, el = volley-ball

Volver (ue) = to return

Vosotros/as = you (pl.)

Voy (from *ir*) = I am going

Vuelve: see *volver (ue)*

Vuestro = your

Wáter, el = lavatory

Windsurfing, el = windsurfing

Y = and

Y cuarto = quarter past

Y media = half past

Y pico = about (with time)

Ya = already

Ya que = since, as

Yo = I; (*soy yo* = it's me)

Yogur, el = yoghurt

Zona, la = zone, area

Zoo, el = zoo

Zumo, el = juice

Vocabulario: inglés – español

A = *un, una*
Able, to be = *poder (ue)*
About (with time) = *sobre; y pico*
Above = *arriba, sobre*
Academy = *academia, la*
Accent = *acento, el*
Accompany, to = *acompañar*
According to = *según*
Accustomed, to be = *soler*
Active = *activo*
Activity = *actividad, la*
Add, to = *añadir*
Address = *dirección, la*
Adequate = *adecuado*
Adjective = *adjetivo, el*
Affectionate = *cariñoso*
After = *después de*
Afternoon = *tarde, la*
Afterwards = *después*
Again = *otra vez*
Age = *edad, la*
Agreed! = *¡de acuerdo!*
Agreement = *acuerdo, el*
Agricultural = *agrario*
Agriculture = *agricultura, la*
All = *todo*
Allow, to = *permitir; dejar*
Almost = *casi*
Along = *por*
Alphabet = *alfabeto, el*
Already = *ya*
Also = *también*
Always = *siempre*
America, United States of = *Estados Unidos, los*
American = *americano*
Amusing = *divertido*
And = *y*
And a bit = *y pico*
Angry = *furioso*
Animal = *animal, el*
Annoying = *pesado*
Anorak = *anorak, el*
Answer = *respuesta, la*
Answer, to = *contestar*
Anthropology = *antropología, la*
Apart (adverb) = *aparte*

Appear (seem), to = *parecer*
Appropriate = *adecuado*
April = *abril*
Aquatic = *acuático*
Area = *zona, la*
Argentina = *Argentina (fem.)*
Argentinian = *argentino*
Armchair = *butaca, la*
Around (time) = *sobre; y pico; a eso de*
Arrive, to = *llegar*
Art = *arte, el; dibujo, el*
Article = *artículo, el*
As = *como*
As a first course = *de primer plato*
As a general rule = *por regla general*
As a main course = *de segundo*
Ask (a question), to = *preguntar*
Ask for, to = *pedir (i)*
Aspirin = *aspirina, la*
At = *a*
At all = *nada*
At home = *en casa*
At once = *en seguida*
At one o'clock = *a la una*
At the end of = *al fin de*
At two o'clock = *a las dos*
Athletics = *atletismo, el*
Attempt, to = *intentar*
August = *agosto*
Aunt = *tía, la*
Australia = *Australia (fem.)*
Australian = *australiano*
Autumn = *otoño, el*
Awful = *fatal*
Bad = *malo* (*mal* before masc. sing. noun)
Bad at, I am = *se me da(n) fatal*
Bad thing, the = *lo malo*
Bad weather, it is = *hace mal tiempo, hace malo*
Bakery = *panadería, la*
Balanced = *equilibrado*
Bank = *banco, el*
Bar = *bar, el*
Barbarism = *barbaridad, la*
Basin = *lavabo, el*
Basketball = *baloncesto, el*
Bath = *bañera, la*

Bath, to have a = *bañarse*

Bathroom = *cuarto de baño, el; baño el*

Be x years old, to = *tener x años*

Be, to = *ser; estar*

Be born, to = *nacer*

Be going to do, to = *ir a* (+ infin.)

Beach = *playa, la*

Because = *porque*

Become, to = *hacerse; ponerse*

Bed = *cama, la*

Bed, to go to = *acostarse (ue)*

Bedroom = *dormitorio, el*

Bedside table = *mesita de noche, la*

Beef = *ternera, la*

Beer = *cerveza, la*

Before (adverb) = *antes*

Before (preposition) = *antes de*

Before -ing = *antes de* (+ infin.)

Begin, to = *comenzar (ie); empezar (ie)*

Behind = *detrás de*

Belgian = *belga*

Belgium = *Bélgica* (fem.)

Believe, to = *creer*

Best = *mejor*

Best wishes = *saludos; un abrazo*

Better = *mejor*

Between = *entre*

Bicycle = *bicicleta, la*

Big = *grande*

Bigger, biggest = *mayor*

Biology = *biología, la*

Bird = *pájaro, el*

Biro = *bolígrafo, el*

Birth = *nacimiento, el*

Birthday = *cumpleaños, el*

Biscuit = *galleta, la*

Black = *negro*

Blackboard = *pizarra, la*

Blank, gap = *hueco, el*

Blonde = *rubio*

Blue = *azul*

Bolivia = *Bolivia* (fem.)

Bon apetit! = *¡que aproveche!*

Book = *libro, el*

Bookcase = *estantería, la*

Border with, to = *limitar con*

Bore = *rollo, el*

Boring = *aburrido*

Born, he/she was = *nació*

Boxing Day = *el 26 de diciembre*

Boy = *chico, el; niño, el*

Boyfriend = *novio, el*

Brave = *valiente*

Bread = *pan, el*

Break (e.g. in school day) = *recreo, el*

Breakfast, to have = *desayunar*

Bright, clear = *claro*

Brilliant = *fenomenal*

Brochure = *folleto, el*

Brother = *hermano, el*

Brown = *marrón*

Brush one's teeth, to = *limpiarse los dientes*

Build, to = *construir*

Building = *edificio, el*

Bull = *toro, el*

Bullfight = *corrida, la; toros, los; corrida de toros, la*

Bullfight, to = *lidiar; torear*

Bullring = *plaza de toros, la*

Bun = *bollo, el*

Bus = *autobús, el*

Bushy = *poblado*

But = *pero*

Buy, to = *comprar*

By car = *en coche*

Café = *cafetería, la*

Calculator = *calculadora, la*

Calibre = *calibre, el*

Called, to be = *llamarse ; apellidarse*

Canada = *Canadá* (masc.)

Canaries = *Las Canarias*

Canteen = *cantina, la*

Cap = *gorro, el*

Cape = *muleta, la*

Capital (city) = *capital, la*

Car = *coche, el*

Card (playing) = *carta, la*

Care = *cuidado, el*

Caretaker = *conserje, el*

Caribbean (adj.) = *caribeño*

Caribbean (Sea) = *(Mar) Caribe, el*

Carpet = *alfombra, la*

Carry, to = *llevar*

Castilian (language) = *castellano*

Castle = *Castillo, el*

Cat = *gato, el*

Catalan = *catalán*

Cathedral = *catedral, la*

CD, CD player = *compact disc, el*

Ceiling = *techo, el*

Celebrate, to = *celebrar*
Celebrity, important person = *personaje, el*
Central America = *Centroamérica* (fem.)
Centre = *centro, el*
Cereals = *cereales, los*
Certain = *seguro*
Chair = *silla, la*
Champagne = *cava, el*
Champion = *campeón, el*
Change = *cambiar*
Chapel = *capilla, la*
Character (e.g. in a book) = *personaje, el*
Chart = *tabla, la*
Chat, to = *charlar*
Cheap = *barato*
Cheese = *queso, el*
Chemistry = *química, la*
Chemist (pharmacy) = *farmacia, la*
Chess = *ajedrez, el*
Chestnut-coloured = *castaño*
Chicken = *pollo, el*
Chickpea = *garbanzo, el*
Chile = *Chile* (masc.)
Chilean = *chileno*
China = *China* (fem.)
Chinese = *chino*
Chips = *patatas fritas, las*
Chocolate = *chocolate, el*
Choose, to = *elegir*
Christmas = *Navidad, la*
Christmas Day = *Día de Navidad, el*
Christmas Eve = *Nochebuena, la*
Church = *iglesia, la*
Cigarette = *cigarillo, el*
Cinema = *cine, el*
City = *ciudad, la*
Class = *clase, la*
Classical = *clásico*
Classroom = *aula* (fem.), *el; clase, la*
Clear = *despejado; claro*
Clear patches = *claros, los*
Clear, to be = *estar despejado*
Climate = *clima, el*
Clock = *reloj, el*
Close (to) = *cerca (de)*
Clothes = *ropa, la*
Cloudy = *nublado*
Cloudy, to be = *estar nublado*
Club = *club, el*
Coast = *costa, la*

Cocoa = *cacao, el*
Coffee (white) = *café (con leche), el*
Coke = *Coca Cola, la*
Cold (very), to be = *hacer (mucho) frio*
Colour = *color, el*
Columbia = *Colombia* (fem.)
Columbian = *colombiano*
Column = *columna, la*
Comb one's hair, to = *peinarse*
Come off it! = *¡anda!*
Come on! = *¡venga!*
Comfortable = *cómodo*
Commentary = *comentario, el*
Companion = *compañero/a, el/la*
Compare, to = *comparar*
Compass = *brújula la*
Complete = *completo*
Complete, to = *completar*
Compulsory = *obligatario*
Computer = *ordenador, el*
Computer Studies = *informática, la*
Concert = *concierto, el*
Consist of, to = *consistir en*
Content = *contento*
Continue, to = *seguir (i)*(1st person sing. = *sigo*)
Continuous = *continuo*
Conversation = *conversación, la*
Cook = *cocinero, el*
Cook, to = *cocer (ue); cocinar*
Cooked in garlic = *al ajillo*
Cooked in salt = *a la sal*
Cool (colloquial) = *chulo; guay*
Cool down, to = *refrescarse*
Cool/chilly, to be = *hacer fresco*
Corner (of street/road) = *esquina, la*
Correct = *correcto*
Correct, to = *corregir (i)*
Corresponding = *correspondiente*
Costa Rica = *Costa Rica* (fem.)
Cotton = *algodón, el*
Country = *país, el*
Countryside = *campo, el; paisaje, el*
Course (of a meal) = *plato, el*
Courtyard = *patio, el*
Cousin (female) = *prima, la*
Cousin (male) = *primo, el*
Cover, to = *tapar*
Cow = *vaca, la*
Cravat = *corbata, la*
Crazy about, to be = *chiflarse*

Cream = *nata, la*
Crop = *cultivo, el*
Cross, to = *cruzar*
Crown = *corona, la*
Cuban = *cubano*
Cultured = *educado*
Cupboard = *armario, el*
Curiosity = *curiosidad, la*
Curly = *rizado*
Currency = *moneda, la*
Cut, to = *cortar*
Cycling = *ciclismo, el*
Dad, Daddy = *papá*
Daily = *diario*
Dance, to = *bailar*
Danish = *danés*
Dark (colour) = *moreno*
Date = *fecha, la*
Daughter = *hija, la*
Dawn = *madruga, la*
Day = *día, el*
Day after tomorrow = *pasado mañana*
December = *diciembre*
Decide, to = *decidir*
Degree = *grado, el*
Degrees, it is x = *hace x grados*
Delicious = *riquísimo; para chuparse los dedos*
Denmark = *Dinamarca* (fem.)
Describe, to = *describir*
Description = *descripción, la*
Desk = *pupitre, el*
Dessert, pudding = *postre, el*
Dialogue = *diálogo, el*
Dictionary = *diccionario, el*
Diet = *dieta, la*
Different = *diferente*
Dining room = *comedor, el; cantina, la*
Dinner = *cena, la*
Dinner, to have = *cenar*
Dirty = *sucio*
Disciplined = *disciplinado*
Discotheque = *discoteca, la*
Discover, to = *descubrir*
Dish, course = *plato, el*
Dishwasher = *lavaplatos, el*
Divide, to = *dividir*
Divided = *dividido*
Do, to = *hacer* (irreg.)
Do (e.g. a sport), to = *practicar*
Doctor = *médico, el*

Dog = *perro, el*
Donkey = *burro, el*
Donut = *donut, el*
Door = *puerta, la*
Draw, to = *dibujar*
Drawing = *dibujo, el*
Drink = *bebida, la*
Drink, to = *beber*
Drink, to have a = *tomar algo*
Dry = *seco*
During = *durante*
Dutch = *holandés*
Each = *cada*
Ear = *oreja, la*
Early = *temprano*
Early evening = *tarde, la*
Earth, ground = *tierra, la*
Easily = *fácilmente*
East = *este, el*
Easy = *fácil*
Eat, to = *comer*
Economy = *economía, la*
Ecuador = *Ecuador* (masc.)
Eight = *ocho*
Eight hundred = *ochocientos*
Eighteen = *dieciocho*
Eighth = *octavo*
Eighty = *ochenta*
El Salvador = *El Salvador* (masc.)
Eleven = *once*
E-mail = *correo electrónico, el; e-mail, el; emilio, el* (slang)
End = *fin, el*
End of = *final de, el*
England = *Inglaterra* (fem.)
English = *inglés*
English (the language) = *inglés, el*
Enjoy your meal! = *¡que aproveche!*
Enough = *bastante; suficiente*
Enter, to = *entrar*
Equals (=) = *son* (from *ser*)
Equipment = *equipo, el*
Especially = *especialmente; sobre todo*
Ethics = *ética, la*
Euro = *euro, el*
Even = *hasta*
Evening (early) = *tarde, la*
Evening (late) = *noche, la*
Every = *cada; todo*
Everybody = *todo el mundo*

Exactly = *exactamente*
Exam = *examen, el*
Example = *ejemplo, el*
Except (for) = *excepto*
Excuse me = *oiga; perdone*
Exercise = *ejercicio, el*
Exercise book = *cuaderno, el*
Explain, to = *explicar*
Explosive = *explosivo, el*
Eye = *ojo, el*
Eye-brow = *ceja, la*
Face = *cara, la*
Fail (of an examination), to = *suspender*
Fair (market, show) = *feria, la*
Fair-skinned = *rubio*
Fall, to = *caer*
False = *falso*
Family = *familia, la*
Famous = *famoso*
Fan, supporter = *aficionado, el*
Fantastic = *fantástico*
Far (from) = *lejos (de)*
Farm = *granja, la*
Fat = *gordo*
Father = *padre, el*
Favourite = *favorito; preferido*
Fear = *miedo, el*
February = *febrero*
Fed up, to be = *harto, estar*
Festival = *fiesta, la*
Field = *campo, el*
Fifteen = *quince*
Fifth = *quinto*
Fifty = *cincuenta*
File, folder = *carpeta, la*
Fill in, to = *rellenar*
Fillet = *filete, el*
Film = *película, la*
Find, to = *encontrar*
Fine, alright = *bien*
Fine weather, it is = *hace buen tiempo, hace bueno*
Finger = *dedo, el*
Finish, to = *terminar*
Finland = *Finlandia* (fem.)
Finnish = *finlandés*
First = *primero* (*primer* before masc. sing. noun)
First course (of meal) = *primer plato, el*
Fish = *pescado, el; pez, el* (plural *peces*)
Five = *cinco*

Five hundred = *quinientos*
Fix, to = *arreglar*
Fizzy = *con gas*
Flavoursome = *sobroso*
Flesh = *carne, la*
Floor (of building) = *planta, la; piso, el*
Floor (of room) = *suelo, el*
Flower = *flor, la*
Fog = *niebla, la*
Foggy, it is = *hay niebla*
Folder, file = *carpeta, la*
Follow, to = *seguir (i)*(1st person sing. = *sigo*)
Following = *siguiente*
Food = *comida, la*
Football = *fútbol, el*
Football (indoor) = *fútbol sala, el*
Football match = *partido de fútbol, el*
For = *para; por*
For example = *por ejemplo*
For the first time = *por primera vez*
For this reason = *por este motivo*
Foreign = *extranjero*
Foreigner = *extranjero, el*
Forget, to = *olvidar*
Form, record-card = *ficha, la*
Forty = *cuarenta*
Four = *cuatro*
Four hundred = *cuatrocientos*
Fourth = *cuarto*
France = *Francia* (fem.)
Free = *libre*
Freezer = *congelador, el*
French = *francés*
French (language) = *francés, el*
Fresh, cool = *fresco*
Friday = *viernes*
Fridge = *nevera, la*
Friend (fem.) = *amiga, la*
Friend (masc.) = *amigo, el*
From = *desde; de*
From time to time = *de vez en cuando*
Frost = *escarcha, la*
Frosty, it is = *hay escarcha*
Frozen = *helado*
Fruit = *fruta, la*
Fun = *divertido*
Funny = *divertido*
Furious = *furioso*
Furniture = *muebles, los*
Fussy = *especial*

Game = *juego, el*
Game, match = *partido, el*
Games, sports = *deportes, los*
Gap = *hueco, el*
Garden = *jardín, el*
Garlic = *ajo, el*
Gas = *gas, el*
General = *general*
Generally = *en general*
Geography = *geografía, la*
German = *alemán*
German (the language) = *alemán, el*
German Shepherd (dog) = *pastor alemán, el*
Germany = *Alemania* (fem.)
Get dressed, to = *vestirse (i)*
Get on well with, to = *llevarse bien con*
Get oneself ready, to = *prepararse; arreglarse*
Get undressed, to = *quitarse la ropa*
Get up, to = *levantarse*
Gibraltar, from = *gibraltareño*
Girl = *chica, la; niña, la*
Girlfriend = *novia, la*
Give, to = *dar*
Glass = *vaso, el*
Go! = *¡id!/¡ve!* (sing.); *¡vaya!/¡vayan!* (pl.)
Go, to = *ir* (irreg)
Go down, to = *bajar*
Go in, to = *entrar*
Go out, to = *salir* (1st pers. sing. = *salgo*)
Go sailing, to = *hacer vela*
Go shopping, to = *ir de tiendas, ir de compras*
Go to bed, to = *acostarse (ue)*
Go up, to = *subir*
Going to do (simple future) = *ir a* (+ infin.)
Gold (the metal) = *oro, el*
Gold (the colour) = *dorado*
Golf = *golf, el*
Good = *bueno* (*buen* before masc. sing. noun)
Good afternoon = *buenas tardes*
Good at, to be = *darse bien; ser fuerte en*
Good morning = *buenos días*
Good night = *buenas noches*
Good thing, the = *lo bueno*
Goodbye = *adiós*
Grand-daughter = *nieta, la*
Grandfather = *abuelo, el*
Grandmother = *abuela, la*
Grandson = *nieto, el*
Grass = *hierba, la*
Great, fantastic (informal) = *guay; genial; magnífico*

Greece = *Grecia* (fem.)
Greek = *griego*
Green = *verde*
Greetings = *saludos*
Grey = *gris*
Grill = *parrilla, la*
Ground, earth = *tierra, la*
Guatemala = *Guatemala* (fem.)
Guess, to = *adivinar*
Guitar = *guitarra, la*
Gulf = *golfo, el*
Gym = *gimnasia, la*
Hair = *pelo, el*
Hake (fish) = *merluza, la*
Half = *medio*
Half past = *y media*
Hall = *vestíbulo, el*
Ham = *jamón, el*
Hammock = *hamaca, la*
Hamster = *hámster, el*
Hand = *mano, la*
Handball = *balonmano, el*
Handsome = *guapo*
Hang out, to = *tender (ie)*
Happy = *feliz*
Hardworking = *trabajador*
Have, to = *tener (ie)* (1st person sing. = *tengo*)
Have a bath, to = *bañarse*
Have a good time, to = *pasarlo bien; pasarlo bomba*
Have a shower, to = *ducharse*
Have a snack, to = *merendar (ie)*
Have breakfast, to = *desayunar*
Have dinner, to = *cenar*
Have lunch, to = *almorzar (ue)*
Have to (be obliged), to = *tener que* (+ infin.)
He = *él*
Head = *cabeza, la*
Headteacher (female) = *directora, la*
Headteacher (male) = *director, el*
Healthy = *sano*
Heat = *calor, el*
Helicopter = *helicóptero, el*
Hello = *hola*
Help, to = *ayudar*
Her/his = *su(s)*
Here = *aquí*
Here are = *aquí están*
Here is = *aquí está*
Hi = *hola*

Highest (top, maximum) = *máximo*
Him, to him = *le*
Himself/herself (reflexive pronoun) = *se*
His/her = *su(s)*
Hispanic = *hispano*
History = *historia, la*
Hobby = *pasatiempo, el*
Holiday (single day) = *día de fiesta, el; día festivo, el*
Holidays (period) = *vacaciones, las*
Holland = *Holanda* (fem.)
Holy week (Easter) = *Semana Santa, la*
Home = *casa, la*
Home, at = *en casa*
Homework = *deberes, los*
Honduras = *Honduras* (masc.)
Horrible = *antipático; horrible*
Horse = *caballo, el*
Horse, to ride a = *montar a caballo; practicar la equitación*
Horse riding = *equitación, la*
Hospital = *hospital, el*
Hot = *caliente*
Hot, to be (very) = *hacer (mucho) calor*
Hotel = *hotel, el*
Hour = *hora, la*
House = *casa, la*
Housewife = *ama (fem.) de casa, el*
How are you? = *¿qué tal?*
How do I get to? = *¿por dónde se va a?*
How lucky = *qué suerte*
How many? = *¿cuántos/as?*
How much? = *¿cuánto/a?*
How nice! = *¡qué gusto!*
How scary = *qué miedo*
How? = *¿cómo?*
However = *sin embargo*
How's it going? = *¿qué hay?*
Hug, embrace = *abrazo, el*
Hundred = *cien(to)*
Hunger = *hambre (fem.), el*
Husband = *marido, el*
I = *yo*
I am = *soy (from ser)*
I hope you get better = *que te mejores*
I.e. = *o sea; es decir*
Ice = *hielo, el*
Ice-cream = *helado, el*
ICT = *informática, la*
Icy, it is = *hay hielo*

Idol = *ídolo, el*
If = *si*
Illustrated = *ilustrado*
Image = *imagen, la*
I'm sorry = *lo siento*
Imperative = *imperativo, el*
Important = *importante*
In = *en*
In a moment, right away = *en seguida*
In front of = *delante de*
In order to = *para/por* (+ infin.)
In total = *en total*
Incredible = *increíble*
India = *India (la)*
Indian = *indio*
Infinitive = *infinitivo, el*
Information = *información, la*
Inhabitant = *habitante, el/la*
Inhuman = *inhumano*
Instruction = *instrucción, la*
Intelligent = *inteligente*
Interesting = *interesante*
Interview = *entrevista, la*
Interview, to = *entrevistar*
Invent, to = *inventar*
Ireland = *Irlanda* (fem.)
Irish = *irlandés*
Iron gate = *cancela, la*
Isle, island = *isla, la*
Issued = *expedido*
It (direct object pronoun) = *lo*
Italian = *italiano*
Italy = *Italia* (fem.)
Jacket = *chaqueta, la*
January = *enero*
Japan = *Japón* (masc.)
Japanese = *japonés*
Jar = *jarra, la*
Jogging = *footing, el*
Journey = *viaje, el*
Judgement, in my = *a mi juicio*
Juice = *zumo, el*
July = *julio*
June = *junio*
Just = *justo*
Keep fit, to = *mantenerse en forma*
Kill, to = *matar*
Kilometre = *kilómetro, el*
Kind, nice = *simpático*
King = *rey, el*

Kitchen = *cocina, la*
Know, to = *saber*
Know (a person or place), to = *conocer*
Laboratory = *laboratorio, el*
Lamb = *cordero, el*
Lamp = *lámpara, la*
Landscape = *paisaje, el*
Language = *idioma, el; lengua, la*
Last (endure), to = *durar*
Late = *tarde*
Latin = *latín, el*
Lavatory = *wáter, el*
Lazy = *perezoso; vago*
Learn, to = *aprender*
Leave, to = *dejar*
Left (as opposed to right) = *izquierda*
Lemon = *limón, el*
Less = *menos*
Let's go = *vamos* (from *ir*)
Letter (missive) = *carta, la*
Library = *biblioteca, la*
Lie = *mentira, la*
Lie (tell a lie), to = *mentir (ie)*
Life = *vida, la*
Light = *luz, la (pl. luces)*
Light (adj.) = *ligero*
Lightning = *rayo, el*
Like = *como*
Like that = *así*
Lion = *león, el*
Listen, to = *escuchar*
Literature = *literatura, la*
Little (amount) = *poco, el*
Live, to = *vivir*
Living room = *sala de estar, la; salón, el*
Location = *localidad, la*
Lock = *cerradura, la*
Lock up, to = *encerrar*
London = *Londres*
Long = *largo*
Look at, to = *mirar*
Look for, to = *buscar*
Lose, to = *perder (ie)*
Loser = *vencido, el*
Lot of, a = *muchos/as*
Love, to = *encantar; chiflar* (both work like *gustar*)
Loving = *cariñoso*
Lunch = *comida, la; almuerzo, el*
Lunch, to have = *almorzar (ue)*

Madam = *señora*
Madrid, from = *madrileño*
Magazine = *revista, la*
Main = *principal*
Main course (of meal) = *segundo plato, el*
Maintenance = *mantenimiento, el*
Make sense, to = *tener sentido*
Make, to = *hacer* (irreg.)
Man = *hombre, el*
Many = *muchos/as*
Map = *mapa, el*
March = *marzo*
Marker pen = *rotulador, el*
Market = *mercado, el*
Market square = *plaza, la*
Marzipan = *mazapán, el*
Mass = *misa, la*
Matador = *matador, el*
Matador, to become a = *tomar la alternativa*
Match up, to = *emparejar*
Match, game = *partido, el*
Maths = *matemáticas, las*
Matter, it doesn't = *no importa*
May = *mayo*
Maybe = *quizá(s)*
Me, to me = *me*
Meal = *comida, la*
Meat = *carne, la*
Meet, to = *encontrar (ue)*
Mention, to = *mencionar*
Mess = *rollo, el*
Metre = *metro, el*
Mexican = *mexicano, mejicano*
Mexico = *Méjico* (masc.)
Midsummer's Day = *Fiesta de San Juan, la*
Mild = *suave*
Milk = *leche, la*
Milkshake = *batido, el*
Million = *millón, el*
Mime = *mimo, el*
Mine = *mina, la*
Mineral = *mineral*
Mining (adj.) = *minero*
Mining (noun) = *minería, la*
Minus (-) = *menos*
Minute = *minuto, el*
Mirror = *espejo, el*
Miss = *señorita*
Mixed = *mixto*
Modern = *moderno*

Moment = *momento, el*
Monday = *lunes*
Month = *mes, el*
More = *más*
Morning = *mañana, la*
Morning, in the (tomorrow) = *mañana*
Morning, early (dawn) = *madrugada, la*
Most = *más*
Mother = *madre, la*
Mountain = *montaña, la*
Mountain range = *sierra, la*
Mouse = *ratón, el*
Mr and Mrs X = *los señores x*
Mr = *señor*
Mrs = *señora*
Much = *mucho*
Multiplied = *multiplicado*
Multiply, to = *multiplicar*
Mum, mummy = *mamá*
Municipal = *municipal*
Museum = *museo, el*
Music = *música, la*
My = *mi(s)*
Myself = *me*
Name = *nombre, el*
Nationality = *nacionalidad, la*
Nativity scene = *belén, el*
Natural = *natural*
Near (to) = *cerca (de)*
Necessary = *necesario*
Neighbour = *vecino/a, el/la*
Neither...nor = *ni...ni*
Never = *nunca*
New = *nuevo*
New Year's Day = *día de Año Nuevo, el*
New Year's Eve = *Nochevieja, la*
Newspaper = *periódico, el*
Next = *próximo*
Next (i.e. that is coming) = *que viene*
Next to = *al lado de*
Next year = *año que viene, el*
Nicaragua = *Nicaragua* (fem.)
Nice = *simpático*
Nickname = *apodo, el*
Night = *noche, la*
Nine = *nueve*
Nine hundred = *novecientos*
Nineteen = *diecinueve*
Ninety = *noventa*
Ninth = *noveno*

No = *no*
No way! = *¡qué va!*
No, not any = *ninguno* (*ningún* before masc. sing. noun)
Nocilla (type of chocolate spread) = *nocilla, la*
Noodle = *fideo, el*
Noodle soup = *sopa de fideos, la*
Nor = *ni*
Normally = *normalmente*
Normally: use *soler* (+ infin.)
North = *norte, el*
Norway = *Noruega* (fem.)
Norwegian = *noruego*
Nose = *nariz, la*
Not = *no*
Not at all = *de nada*
Nothing = *nada*
Notice-board = *tablón, el*
Nougat = *turrón, el*
November = *noviembre*
Now = *ahora*
Nowadays = *hoy en día*
Nuisance = *fastidio, el*
Number = *número, el*
Numerous = *numeroso*
O'clock (exactly) = *en punto*
Ocean = *océano, el*
October = *octubre*
Odd job = *chapuza, la*
Of = *de*
Of course = *desde luego; claro*
Office = *oficina, la*
Official = *oficial*
Oil = *petróleo, el*
Okay (satisfactory) = *regular*
Okay? (agree?) = *¿vale?*
Old = *viejo*
Older, oldest = *mayor*
Omelette = *tortilla, la*
On = *en*
On average = *de media*
On foot = *andando*
On the dot = *en punto*
On the way = *de camino*
On the ... hand side = *a mano ...*
On top of = *sobre*
One = *uno*
One has to = *hay que*
Only = *solo; único*
Only child (female) = *hija única, la*

Only child (male) = *hijo único, el*
Open, to = *abrir*
Opinion, in my = *en mi opinión*
Opposite (to) = *enfrente (de)*
Optional = *optativo*
Or = *o*
Orange (the colour) = *naranja*
Orange (the fruit) = *naranja, la*
Order = *orden, el*
Order, to = *mandar*
Origin = *origen, el*
Other = *otro*
Ought, I/he/she = *debería*
Our = *nuestro*
Ourselves = *nos*
Outside = *fuera*
Outskirts = *afueras, las*
Oven = *horno, el*
P.E. (physical education) = *educación física, la*
P.O. Box = *apartado postal (apdo. postal), el*
Pacific = *Pacífico, el*
Paella = *paella, la*
Pagan = *pagano*
Page = *página, la*
Painted = *pintado*
Painter = *pintor, el*
Painting = *cuadro, el*
Panama = *Panamá* (masc.)
Paper; piece of paper = *papel, el*
Paragraph = *párrafo, el*
Paraguay = *Paraguay* (masc.)
Parents = *padres, los*
Park = *parque, el*
Partner = *pareja, la*
Party (celebration) = *fiesta, la*
Pass (an examination), to = *aprobar (ue)*
Pasta = *pasta, la*
Patriotic = *patriótico*
Patron = *patrona, la*
Pedestrian = *peatón, el*
Pen = *bolígrafo, el*
Pencil = *lápiz, el*
Pencil sharpener = *sacapuntas, el*
Pencil-case = *estuche, el*
Peninsula = *península, la*
People = *gente, la* (used in singular)
Perfect = *perfecto*
Perform, to = *actuar*
Perhaps = *quizá(s)*
Person = *persona, la*

Peru = *Perú* (masc.)
Peso (unit of currency in S. America) = *peso, el*
Pet = *mascota, la; animal, el*
Physics = *física, la*
Picture = *dibujo, el*
Pink = *rosa*
Pizza = *pizza, la*
Place = *sitio, el*
Plan = *plano, el*
Planet = *planeta, el*
Play (a game), to = *jugar*
Play (a musical instrument), to = *tocar*
Pleasant = *agradable*
Please = *por favor*
Please, to = *gustar*
Plus (+) = *más*
Point out, to = *indicar*
Polite, cultured = *educado*
Poor = *pobre*
Pop (short for popular) = *pop*
Popular = *popular*
Pork = *cerdo, el*
Portugal = *Portugal* (masc.)
Portuguese = *portugués*
Position = *posición, la*
Possess, to = *poseer*
Post office = *Correos*
Poster = *póster, el*
Potato = *patata, la*
Practise, to = *practicar*
Pram = *cochecito de niño, el*
Pray, to = *orar; rezar*
Praying Mantis = *mantis religiosa, la*
Prefer, to = *preferir (ie)*
Prepare oneself, to = *prepararse*
Prepare, to = *preparar*
Present (adj.) = *presente*
Present (gift) = *regalo, el*
Present (tense) = *presente, el*
Present, to = *presentar*
Pretty = *guapo; bonito*
Primary = *primario*
Private = *privado*
Probably = *a lo mejor*
Problem = *problema, el*
Producer = *productor, el*
Programme = *programa, el*
Projector = *proyector, el*
Pronoun = *pronombre, el*
Pronounce, to = *pronunciar*

Province = *provincia, la*
Pudding = *postre, el*
Pupil = *alumno/a, el/la*
Purple = *morado*
Push, to = *empujar*
Put, to = *meter; poner*
Pyramid = *pirámide, la*
Quarter = *cuarto, el*
Quarter past = *y cuarto*
Quarter to = *menos cuarto*
Queen = *reina, la*
Question = *pregunta, la*
Quickly, promptly = *pronto*
Quiet, to be = *callarse*
Quite, enough = *bastante*
Rabbit = *conejo, el*
Radio = *radio, la*
Rain = *precipitaciones, las*
Rain, to = *llover (ue)*
Rainy = *lluvioso*
Rainy weather = *tiempo lluvioso*
Rarely = *con poca frecuencia*
Reach (go up to), to = *alcanzar*
Reach the age of, to = *cumplir*
Read, to = *leer*
Reading = *lectura, la*
Real = *real*
Really = *mucho; realmente*
Reason = *razón, la*
Receive, to = *recibir*
Record-card = *ficha, la*
Red = *rojo*
Red (of wine) = *tinto*
Red-haired, ginger = *pelirrojo*
Reflexive = *reflexivo*
Region = *región, la*
Relax, to = *relajarse*
Religious Studies, R.E. = *religión, la*
Remember, to = *acordarse (ue)*
Represented = *representado*
Residence = *domicilio, el*
Responsible = *responsable*
Restaurant = *restaurante, el*
Return, to = *regresar; volver (ue)*
Revision = *repaso, el*
Ride a bike, to = *montar en bici(cleta)*
Ride a horse, to = *montar a caballo; practicar la equitación*
Right (as opposed to wrong) = *justo*
Right (as opposed to left) = *derecho*

Right away = *en seguida; ahora mismo*
Road = *carretera, la*
Roof = *tejado, el*
Roof-rack = *baca, la*
Room = *sala, la; habitación, la*
Rosé (wine) = *rosado*
Rough = *rudo*
Round = *redondo*
Routine = *rutina, la*
Rubber = *goma, la*
Rucksack, school-bag = *mochilla, la*
Rugby = *rugby, el*
Ruler, rule = *regla, la*
Run, to = *correr*
Russia = *Rusia* (fem.)
Russian = *ruso*
Sailing = *vela, la*
Sailing, to go = *hacer vela*
Sailor = *navegante, el*
Saint = *santo, el*
Salad = *ensalada, la*
Salami = *chorizo, el*
Salami sausage (spicy) = *salchichón, el*
Salt = *sal, la*
Same = *mismo*
Same as = *igual que*
Sandwich = *bocadillo, el*
Saturday = *sábado*
Say, to = *decir (i)*; 1st person singular *digo*
School = *escuela, la*
School (primary) = *colegio, el*
School (secondary) = *instituto, el*
School, of a (adj.) = *escolar*
School-bag = *mochila, la*
Science = *ciencia, la*
Science (the subject) = *ciencias, las*
Scissors = *tijeras, las*
Scotland = *Escocia* (fem.)
Scottish = *escocés*
Scrub, to = *fregar (ie)*
Sea = *mar, el*
Sea bass = *lubina, la*
Sea bream = *besugo, el*
Season = *estación, la*
Second = *segundo*
Second course = *de segundo*
Secretary = *secretaria, la*
Sector = *sector, el*
See you later = *hasta la vista; hasta luego*
See, to = *ver*

Seem, to = *parecer*
Sell, to = *vender*
Send, to = *mandar*
Sense = *sentido, el*
Sentence = *frase, la*
September = *septiembre*
Seven = *siete*
Seven hundred = *setecientos*
Seventeen = *diecisiete*
Seventh = *séptimo*
Seventy = *setenta*
Shack = *chabola, la*
Shandy = *clara, la*
Shape = *forma, la*
Shave, to = *afeitarse*
She = *ella*
Shellfish = *mariscos, los*
Shop = *tienda, la*
Shopping = *compra, la*
Shopping, to go = *ir de tiendas, ir de compras*
Short (height) = *bajo*
Short (length) = *corto*
Shower = *ducha, la*
Shower, to have a = *ducharse*
Showers (rainfall) = *chubascos, los*
Shut, to = *encerrar*
Side = *lado, el*
Sight = *vista, la*
Silver (the metal) = *plata, la*
Silver (the colour) = *plateado*
Similar = *parecido*
Sink = *fregadero, el*
Sir = *señor*
Sister = *hermana, la*
Sit down, to = *sentarse (ie)*
Situated = *situado*
Six = *seis*
Six hundred = *seiscientos*
Sixth = *sexto*
Sixty = *sesenta*
Size = *tamaño, el*
Skate, to = *patinar*
Skating = *patinaje, el*
Ski, to = *esquiar*
Skiing = *esquí, el*
Skin = *piel, la*
Skirt = *falda, la*
Sky = *cielo, el*
Sleep, to = *dormir (ue)*
Sleepy, to be = *tener sueño*

Slow = *despacio*
Small = *pequeño*
Smaller = *menor*
Smoke, to = *fumar*
Snack = *merienda, la*
Snow = *nieve, la*
Snow, to = *nevar (ie)*
So = *tan*
So much = *tanto*
So then = *así que*
Soap = *jabón, el*
Soap-opera (TV) = *telenovela, la*
Socks = *calcetines, los*
Sofa = *sofá, el*
Soft drink = *refresco, el*
Sole (fish) = *lenguado, el*
Solve, to = *solucionar*
Some = *algún, alguna; unos*
Something = *algo*
Sometimes = *a veces; algunas veces*
Son = *hijo, el*
Sorrow, trouble, pain = *pena, la*
Soup = *sopa, la*
South = *sur, el*
South America = *Sudamérica* (fem.)
Southern = *meridional*
Spain = *España* (fem.)
Spanish = *español*
Spanish (the language) = *español, el*
Speak on the telephone, to = *hablar por teléfono*
Speak, to = *hablar*
Special = *especial*
Spectacle = *espectáculo, el*
Speech = *discurso, el*
Spell out, to = *deletrear*
Spider = *araña, la*
Sport (one only) = *deporte, el*
Sports (generally) = *deportes, los*
Sports centre, sports hall = *polideportivo, el*
Sporty = *deportista; deportivo*
Spring = *primavera, la*
Square (of a town) = *plaza, la*
Squash = *squash, el*
Stadium = *estadio, el*
Staff room = *sala de profesores, la*
Start, to = *empezar (ie)*
Station = *estación, la*
Stay at home, to = *quedarse en casa*
Step-brother = *hermanastro, el*
Step-father = *padrastro, el*

Step-mother = *madrastra, la*
Step-sister = *hermanastra, la*
Stereotype = *estereotipo, el*
Stew = *cocido, el*
Still (non-fizzy) = *sin gas*
Still, yet = *todavía*
Storm = *tormenta, la*
Stormy, it is = *hay tormenta*
Story = *historia, la*
Straight = *recto*
Straight ahead = *todo recto*
Street = *calle, la*
Strong = *valiente, fuerte*
Student = *estudiante, el/la*
Study, to = *estudiar*
Stupid = *imbécil*
Subject (school) = *asignatura, la*
Suck, to = *chupar*
Sufficient = *suficiente*
Sufficient, to be = *bastar*
Sugar = *azúcar, el/la*
Summer = *verano, el*
Sun = *sol, el*
Sunday = *domingo*
Sunny = *soleado*
Sunny weather = *tiempo soleado*
Sunny, to be = *hacer sol*
Super, great (informal) = *guay*
Superb = *magnífico; estupendo*
Supermarket = *supermercado, el*
Supporter, fan = *aficionado, el*
Sure, certain = *seguro*
Surf (e.g. the internet), to = *navegar*
Surname = *apellido, el*
Survey = *encuesta, la*
Swap around, change roles = *cambia de papel*
Swedish = *sueco*
Sweden = *Suecia* (fem.)
Swim, to = *nadar*
Swim, to have a = *bañarse*
Swimmer = *nadador, el*
Swimming = *natación, la*
Swimming pool = *piscina, la*
Sword = *espada, la*
Table = *mesa, la*
Take, to = *coger; tomar*
Take (photos), to = *sacar*
Talk, to = *hablar*
Tall = *alto*
Tape = *cinta, la*

Taste = *gusto, el*
Tasty = *sabroso*
teach, to = *enseñar*
Teacher (female) = *profesora, la*
Teacher (male) = *profesor, el*
Team = *partido, el; cuadrilla, la; equipo, el*
Technology = *tecnología, la*
Telephone = *teléfono, el*
Telephone, to = *telefonear*
Telephonic = *telefónico*
Television = *televisión, la*
Tell a lie, to = *mentir (ie)*
Temperature = *temperatura, la*
Ten = *diez*
Tennis = *tenis, el*
Tenth = *décimo*
Textbook = *libro de texto, el*
Thank goodness! = *¡menos mal!*
Thank you very much = *muchas gracias*
Thank you, thanks = *gracias*
That (after a verb) = *que*
That is to say, i.e. = *es decir*
That which = *el que*
That, those (demonstrative adjective) = *ese, esa, esos, esas*
That, those (demonstrative pronoun) = *ése, ésa, ésos, ésas*
That's right = *eso es*
That's to say = *o sea*
That's why = *por eso*
The = *el, la, los, las*
Theatre = *teatro, el*
Their = *su(s)*
Them (direct object pronoun) = *los/las*
Themselves (reflexive pronoun) = *se*
Then, so then = *luego ; entonces*
There (in the distance) = *allá*
There (quite near) = *allí*
There is, there are = *hay*
They = *ellos/as*
Thin = *delgado*
Thing = *cosa, la*
Think, to = *pensar (ie)*
Think that, to = *opinar que; creer que; me parece que*
Third = *tercero*
Thirty = *treinta*
This (one) = *éste/a/o*
This (thing) = *esto*
Thousand = *mil*

Three = *tres*
Three hundred = *trescientos*
Through = *por*
Thursday = *jueves*
Time = *tiempo, el*
Time (occasion) = *vez, la*
Time (of day) = *hora, la*
Time (short period) = *rato, el*
Time, free = *ratos libres, los; tiempo libre, el*
Timetable = *horario, el*
Timid = *tímido*
Tired, (literally: to have sleep) = *estar cansado; tener sueño*
To = *a*
To have a drink = *tomar algo*
Toast = *tostadas, las*
Toasted = *tostado*
Toaster = *tostador, el*
Today = *hoy*
Together = *juntos*
Tomorrow = *mañana*
Too = *también; demasiado*
Tooth = *diente, el*
Top, highest = *máximo*
Tortoise = *tortuga, la*
Torture, to = *martirizar*
Tourist = *turista, el/la*
Tourist information office = *oficina de turismo, la*
Town hall = *ayuntamiento, el*
Town, village = *pueblo, el*
Tradition = *tradición, la*
Traffic-light = *semáforo, el*
Translate, to = *traducir*
Tree = *árbol, el*
Tropical = *tropical*
True = *verdadero*
Truth = *verdad, la*
Try (attempt), to = *intentar*
Tuesday = *Martes*
Turkey (the bird) = *pavo, el*
Turn, to = *doblar; torcer*
Tutorial = *tutoría, la*
TV = *tele, la*
Twelve = *doce*
Twenty = *veinte*
Twist, to = *torcer*
Two = *dos*
Two hundred = *doscientos*
Type = *tipo, el*
Typical = *típico*

Umbrella = *paraguas, el*
Uncle = *tío, el*
Under = *debajo de*
Underline, to = *subrayar*
Understand, to = *comprender*
Undress, to = *quitarse la ropa*
University = *universidad, la*
Unkind = *antipático*
Until = *hasta*
Upstairs = *arriba*
Uruguay = *Uruguay* (masc.)
Us, to us = *nos*
USA = *Estados Unidos, los*
Use, to = *utilizar*
Useful = *útil*
Valid = *válido (val.)*
Varied = *variado*
Various = *vario; diverso*
Vegetables = *verduras, las*
Vegetarian = *vegetariano*
Venezuela = *Venezuela* (fem.)
Verb = *verbo, el*
Very = *muy*
Very well = *muy bien*
Video = *vídeo, el*
Villa = *chalet, el*
Village = *pueblo, el*
Visit, to = *visitar*
Volley-ball = *voleibol, el*
Wake up, to = *despertarse (ie)*
Wales = *Gales* (masc.)
Wall (of a building) = *pared, la*
Want, to = *querer (ie)*
Wardrobe = *armario, el*
Wash oneself, to = *lavarse*
Wash, to = *lavar*
Washing-machine = *lavadora, la*
Watch = *reloj, el*
Watch, to = *mirar*
Water = *agua (fem.), el*
Water sports = *deportes acuáticos, los*
Way = *vía, la*
We = *nosotros/as*
Wear, to = *llevar*
Weather = *tiempo, el*
Weather forecast = *pronóstico del tiempo, el*
Wednesday = *miércoles*
Week = *semana, la*
Weekend = *fin de semana, el*
Weight = *peso, el*

Well (good) = *bien*
Well… (hesitating) = *pues…*
Welsh = *galés*
West = *oeste, el*
What a pain = *qué pesado*
What a shame = *qué pena; ¡vaya!*
What are….like? = *¿cómo son?*
What is….like? = *¿cómo es?*
What? = *¿qué?*
What? = *¿cuál?*
When = *cuando*
When? = *¿cuándo?*
Where = *donde*
Where? = *¿dónde?*
Which? = *¿cuál?*
While = *mientras que*
White = *blanco*
Who (relative pronoun) = *quien*
Who? = *¿quién?*
Why? = *¿por qué?*
Wife = *mujer, la*
Wind = *viento, el*
Window = *ventana, la*
Windsurfing = *windsurfing, el*
Windy, to be = *hacer viento*
Wine = *vino, el*
Winter = *invierno, el*
With = *con*
With you = *contigo*
Witness = *testigo, el*

Woman = *mujer, la*
Wonderful = *estupendo*
Word = *palabra, la*
Work = *trabajo, el*
Work, to = *trabajar*
Working (adj.) = *laboral*
World = *mundo, el*
World, of the (adj) = *mundial*
Worst thing, the = *lo peor*
Would like, I (conditional tense) = *me gustaría*
Write, to = *escribir*
Year = *año, el*
Year (school) = *curso, el*
Yell, to = *gritar*
Yellow = *amarillo*
Yes = *sí*
Yesterday = *ayer*
Yet, still = *todavía*
Yoghurt = *yogur, el*
You (familiar form) = *tú, vosotros/as*
You (polite form) = *usted (vd.), ustedes (vds.)*
You must be joking! = *¡no fastidies!*
Young = *joven*
Younger = *menor*
Your = *tu(s); vuestro*
Yourself = *te*
Yourself (used after prepositions) = *tí* (e.g. *sobre tí* = about yourself)
Yourselves = *os*
Zoo = *zoo, el*

Index of subjects

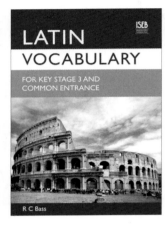
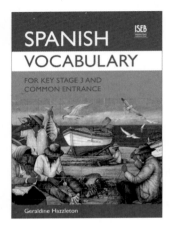